Soccer Tactics 2014

What The World Cup Taught Us

Ray Power

BENNION KEARNY

Academy Soccer Coach is a company that provides digital solutions for coaches at every level of the game.

Our coaching software enables 1000's of coaches, clubs and professional organizations to plan and create their sessions remotely from anywhere in the world.

Academy Soccer Coach works with following the professional clubs and organizations:

Fulham FC, West Ham United FC, Stoke FC, Newcastle United FC, Crystal Palace FC, Burnley FC, The Portland Timbers, Sporting Kansas City, National Soccer Coaches Association of America, USSF Women's National Teams, The Irish Football Association, The Football Association of Ireland, The Professional Footballers Association, and many more.

For more information please visit www.academysoccercoach.com

On a personal note, we would like to wish Ray every success with his book and his continued growth and development as a coach.

The ASC Team

To Lisa – Your help and support means more than you'll ever know. Onto the next chapter.

To Gracie and Georgia – Thank you for allowing me to take over the TV, laptop, and iPad for an entire month of the World Cup!

About the Author

Securing a BA Degree in 2004, Ray went on to qualify as a teacher. Having worked in the classroom environment, Ray took his teaching to the soccer field, working with players of various ages, backgrounds, and within several professional academies in England.

Ray is currently the Academy Manager at Central College and is a Coach Educator with the English Football Association.

Table of Contents

Foreword

Ray Power has done it again! Writing a quality, in-depth, easy-to-read book about football. Something that looks simple to do but which definitely is not. Football is sometimes like a painting of Van Gogh. From a distance you think you have seen the complete picture but the closer you get - the more detail you discover.

Having been fortunate to have worked with Louis van Gaal at the Dutch KNVB and benefitting from his unbelievable attention to tactical detail, I was pleased to recognise a similar analytical attitude when reading this book. During my time at KNVB young Wesley Sneijder, Robin van Persie and Arjen Robben just came and played their game without bothering about tactics. Now, as established world class players, it is very different.

With tactics, a fundamental is whether the Coach asks his players to play the way that suits his philosophy or whether he looks for a philosophy that suits his players. It's a big question. To change the style of play in a country that has a particular culture ingrained can be very counterproductive but can also lead to World Cup success as the Spanish and German have proven over the last 10 years.

Football will always be 11 v 11 wherever in the world we see a game but 1-4-4-2 is sometimes 1-4-4-1-1 and sometimes 1-4-3-1-2. 1-4-3-4 is sometimes 1-4-2-3-1 and sometimes 1-2-3-2-3.

To the fans, it sometimes doesn't make any difference. All they want to see is a fast game with lots of opportunities in and around the box, and a positive result.

In reality tactics can make a significant difference on the pitch and for both coaches and players. Preparing your team and becoming aware of your opponents' strategy and the ability to use the strengths of your players is key for success.

In *Soccer Tactics 2014* - Ray has dissected the World Cup 2014 tactics into specific detailed chapters. It was one of the best World Cups ever, especially due to the diversity of tactics, styles and philosophies, but also thanks to players like James Rodrigues, Arjen Robben, Thomas Muller and Lionel Messi with their exceptional individual qualities. Such players could only excel due to the philosophy and the way the coach had set up his team tactics.

Ray has produced again a quality 'must read' book for all coaches interested in the modern game and the on-going development of football tactics. It is a great addition to his 'Making The Ball Roll' football handbook.

I wish you an enjoyable read!

Mark Wotte, Performance Director Scottish Football Association

Introduction:
Understanding Tactics

"As long as humanity exists something new will come along – otherwise football dies!" (Italian Football Coach and Tactician, Arrigo Sacchi)

For those of us who love football tactics, the landscape of constantly changing styles of play over recent years has left us marvelling. We have looked at the dominant Spain and wondered how they dared to play such an expansive, tiki-taka game. We saw Greece's organised, defensive method achieve glory at the European Championships in 2004 (almost the polar opposite of the tactical approach of the Iberians). We have looked at how Brazil's approach has changed, how Italy has risen and fallen internationally, and wondered whether African or Asian teams could really adopt a way that would see them go all the way in a World Cup.

The 2014 World Cup in Brazil gave the lovers of football tactics even more – and all within the space of 32 days! This tournament will become the backdrop for our analysis of modern football tactics.

Evolution

The only place to begin a book about soccer tactics is by using the above quote from Arrigo Sacchi. The central point in the Italian's quote is about *evolution*. Every aspect of the world evolves as time passes, including football tactics. For example, look at how the role of the traditional 'number 10' has developed in recent years. Following the growth in the number of teams using a defensive midfield player, the number '10' needed to evolve and play elsewhere on the pitch to avoid a defensive player in their zone. The types of players we would normally typecast as a number '10' are now using their technical skills elsewhere on the pitch – the Brazilian Oscar spent much of this World Cup playing as a right-midfielder while Croatia's Luca Modrić played as a deep-lying midfield player.

Introduction

We would also be foolish to think that certain tactics 'die'. They do not. At best, they hibernate only to resurface again when other changes in the game allow them to.

I remember a few years ago when candidates on my UEFA 'A' Licence course shunned the idea of playing with a back three and a sweeper as irrelevant in the modern game. But it has re-emerged in recent years and was a high profile approach at the 2014 World Cup.

When discussing tactics in my first book - *Making the Ball Roll* - I felt it important to point out something I call the "numbers game", and it is something I am keen to do here.

The "Numbers Game"

Throughout this book we will use lots of numbers – we are, after all, talking about football tactics – whether those numbers happen to be 4-2-3-1, 4-4-2, or 3-4-3.

What we must realise, however, is that tactics are much, much more complex than a combination of numbers on a television screen or in our newspaper articles. Tactics, as so clearly explained by Jonathan Wilson in *Inverting the Pyramid*, are "a combination of formation and style" – so, they are a merging of the numbers we use to describe our formation, and the style of football we wish to implement. In addition, tactics are a combination of player strengths, movements, and real decisions taken during the real action of a football game.

Using the numbers as a starting point, and a starting point only, gives you a general outline of a team's shape, but all these shapes can vary. We could spend hours poring over whether Mexico played 3-5-2 or 5-3-2 or whether Cameroon's formation against them was mainly 6-3-1 rather than the 4-3-3 set out on the pre-match team sheet. The French and Russians both played a 4-3-3 formation, but varied considerably in their approach and tactics. So ultimately, while the numbers give us a good basis to start, in the all-action fluency of a football match - they are situational and can adjust at any given point.

Argentina – 4-4-2 Diamond / 4-3-3 / 4-1-2-1-2?

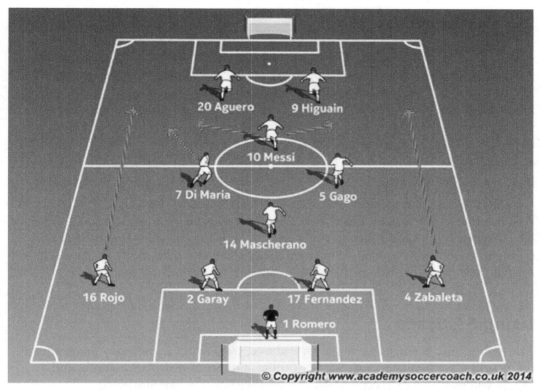

The above diagram is the team shape Argentina utilised in the second half of their opening Group F game against Bosnia, having changed from a 3-5-1-1 at half-time. On paper, we may well call this a 4-4-2 with a diamond midfield, but with Lionel Messi more of an attacker than a midfielder, we can easily label it as 4-3-3. In some places we have also seen this called 4-1-2-1-2. The point is, the numbers used is not the most important thing – rather, it is our understanding of the team's style, patterns, and the decisions of players on the grass.

Absolute Statements

Before we delve into the tactical trends that are shaping modern football, it is worth pausing to take stock of (and, in a sense, put to bed) some myths that have become ingrained in match analysis even from the pundits that we see on our television screens employed purely to provide expert commentary.

Absolute statements are those definitive words like 'always' and 'never'. When I hear such words mentioned in football analysis, I sometimes close one eye and hope that the remaining part of the sentence is at least partly accurate! Often, however, the remaining part of the sentence is not accurate at all. By using absolute terms (such as "always") we are essentially saying that something happened 100% of the time.

Introduction

During the World Cup, Argentina's Mascherano did not complete every tackle, Neymar did not always beat his opponent 1v1, and the notion that the Germans never gave the ball away is incorrect, although media hyperbole and sensationalist newspapers would lead some to believe otherwise.

The group stages of the 2014 World Cup for example produced 136 goals – more goals than for any other World Cup, six more than the previous record-setting 2002 tournament co-hosted by Japan and Korea (source: FIFA). This does not mean however that *all* games were goal-fests. There were several games that ended 0–0 and there were plenty of clean sheets. During the group stages there were goalless draws between Iran and Nigeria, Brazil and Mexico, Japan and Greece, Costa Rica and England, and Ecuador and France. Of the 48 games played during the group phase, there were 21 occasions when games involved at least one team that did not concede.

As can often be customary then, we will steer clear of absolute statements from here on in. When you see one used in other analysis, it is time to question its validity. Germany's trend was to play short from the goalkeeper and build from the back, but they did not *always* do it. Let's base our analysis in fact instead.

Using Statistics

Throughout the book, as we have done above, we will utilise various statistics from the World Cup. I will generate some of these stats from my own research, and others will come from exceptionally informative sources like Squawka, FourFourTwo Stats Zone, Who Scored, Prozone and the resources provided by official FIFA documents (plus other stats published in various articles and assessments of games).

Statistics will be used, where necessary, to help illuminate points, rather than seeking to blind the reader with their application. It is also worth pointing out that statistics are not always necessary. For example, below are two diagrams from Prozone displaying statistics from Dirk Kuyt's performance for the Netherlands in the World Cup semi-final against Argentina. Kuyt played the first half as a right wing-back and the second half as a left wing-back.

Kuyt's Average Positions v. Argentina (after 80 minutes)

Kuyt's Actual Possessions v. Argentina (after 80 minutes)

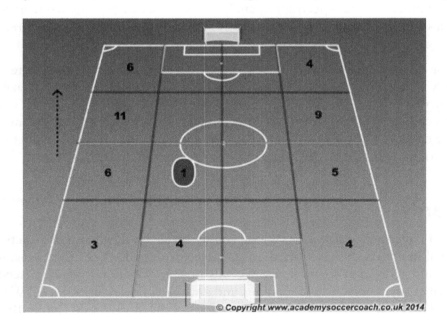

Diagram one shows Kuyt's 'average' position as being right in the middle of the pitch, although diagram two shows the actual areas of the pitch where he had possession. His average position, therefore, is completely inaccurate, considering he only had one individual possession in any of the four midfield areas.

'Winner's' History

They say that history is written by whoever wins the war. In a sense the analysis of football tactics can be the same. We often incorrectly judge whether tactics are effective or not based purely on the final result. If a team wins, their tactics are deemed to be absolutely correct and the tactics of the other team are, more often than not, unjustifiably forgotten about.

Just prior to the quarter-finals of the 2014 World Cup, I had a conversation with a fellow coach who is also exceptionally analytical about football. We were discussing what teams we expected to do well (or not) in the remaining games. During our conversation he stated that he would be reserving his judgment for the success of certain teams once the tournament was over and we knew who had won. Needless to say this started quite a debate!

While Germany, as world champions, will feature heavily in this book (and rightly so), for the holistic legitimacy of the book's content, we will spend a lot of time using examples from teams that made it into the early phases of the knock-out rounds, but also those who exited the competition at the group phase. If we only use history's winners for our spectrum of analysis, we would neglect the wonderful tactical lessons we can still learn from the Netherlands, France, Costa Rica, Iran and Cameroon.

Chile, for example, made it to the last 16 of the competition, where they were ultimately beaten on penalties after an enthralling game against the hosts Brazil. In fact, they were only the width of the crossbar away from winning the match in extra-time. According to our historians, however, they will have exited the tournament at the same stage as Algeria, Greece and Nigeria, and their adventurous, distinct style of play would be forgotten. We will not be forgetting them here.

Onwards

So while I have spent a few pages telling you what this book will not do – here is what it will do! We will look at modern soccer tactics, and look at how the game has changed and evolved in recent times. We will look at formations, systems, trends, positional changes, attacking, defending, and a whole lot more in-between! We will do this all through the lens of the riveting games of the 2014 World Cup in Brazil.

1

Football Tactics
and National Identity

"Surprised to read negative Dutch media about defensive playing style. It's about winning!" (Raymond Verheijen, Dutch Fitness Expert and Football Coach)

All football leagues around the world have teams with different philosophies, a different style of play, and different sub-cultures. We often find that national teams have distinct (sometimes unique) philosophies, play, and cultures. The beauty of World Cup competitions is the convergence of many of these different styles; all in the one place, in a one-month period.

In Brazil, some nations stuck rigidly to their national footballing identities. Some significantly moved away from their cultural roots in the game, while others, possibly still seeking to shape their own national distinctiveness, went about formulating their tactics based on: foreign influence (South Korea), their recent success (Greece), or their perceived failures (England).

Chapter 1

Sticking Firm

There is a great video available on YouTube of a team talk from Pep Guardiola to his Barcelona team before extra-time of their 2009 European Super Cup Final. Even in the tough circumstances of a hard-fought win against Shakhtar Donetsk, he insisted on the team playing the game "our way".[1] It was steadfast, unwavering, and assertive.

Below, we will look at two teams from the 2014 World Cup, whose insistence on doing things "their way" in Brazil would have mixed consequences.

Spain

Before a ball was kicked at the 2014 World Cup, we all wondered whether this generation of Spanish players could emulate their successes from recent international tournaments. Although humbled by hosts Brazil in the Confederations Cup in 2013, a lot was expected of Spain. They had, after all, won three back-to-back international tournaments; their 2010 World Cup victory in South Africa sandwiched between the lifting of European Championship titles in 2008 and 2012.

We all also knew that Vicente del Bosque's side would stick firm with the 'tiki-taka' style of play that had brought them such success. In Brazil, although they lasted a mere three games, they still believed that they would win by dominating the ball, predominantly using short, precise passes and pressing their opponents aggressively. Regardless of their early exit, Spain's average possession from their three games was 61.4% - the highest in the tournament (whoscored.com).

Although the team contained nine of the same starting line-up that lifted the European Championships two years previously (and eight of the team who began the 2010 World Cup Final), questions into a lack of team evolution were always going to need answering.

There were, however, subtle changes to Spain's approach, mainly with the abandonment of their 'False 9' striker system, something they had pioneered in the modern game. In the 2012 European Championships, this role was fulfilled by midfielder Cesc Fàbregas, but was replaced (for 2014) with the Atletico Madrid forward Diego Costa, who played as an out-and-out number 9. Whether this can be looked at as a step forward, in terms of modern tactics, or a step backwards (where a rigid centre-forward replaced a free-flowing false striker) is debatable.

---

[1] This video is available to view at http://www.youtube.com/watch?v=iRhVGSKVYMU

What has been found over the last couple of seasons is that, as football evolves, opponents not only learn how to combat a particular tactical blueprint, but also learn how to combat the same players using the same tactics. More and more teams are now challenging the dominance of tiki-taka, which culminated in two comprehensive Spanish defeats against the Netherlands (5 – 1) and Chile (2 – 0) in their opening games.

Spain's 'False 9' System, European Champions Final, 2012

Spain's starting XI in their 2012 European Championships Final against Italy. Nine of this team started against The Netherlands in the 2014 World Cup, the main difference being their use of Cesc Fàbregas as a 'False 9'.

Spain's 4-2-3-1 v. The Netherlands, 2014

Spain's starting line-up in their opening game, a 5 - 1 defeat against The Netherlands. They stuck with their tried and tested 4-2-3-1 template, but used Diego Costa as a central striker, rather than Fàbregas as their 'False 9'.

Choosing Winning Over Identity

The Chileans were arguably everyone's second favourite team at the 2014 World Cup. Owing much to the influence of renowned former coach Marco Bielsa, who took charge of Chile at the 2010 finals, current coach Jorge Sampiola set about implementing a style that would stay true to the South Americans' recent playing approach.

For the tacticians amongst us, watching Chile was, at times, quite surreal. They played with a high tempo both in and out of possession, attacking and defending as if their footballing lives depended on it. The former Manchester United right-back Gary Neville once commented that it seemed like a ten-year-old with a PlayStation controller was dictating the moves of the often fast-driven, erratic Brazilian, David

Luiz. While watching Chile, one would be forgiven for thinking the same of the team as a whole(!), although there was a lot more craft and team synergy to their play.

Beyond their exciting, quick-tempo play was a tactical structure and organisation that rivalled any other team in Brazil. Apart from their opening game against Australia, they stuck with their three-at-the-back roots that had served Bielsa so well, lining up in a 3-4-1-2 formation, that contained the dangerous front two of Barcelona's Alexis Sanchez, and Napoli's Eduardo Vargas – with Juventus midfielder Arturo Vidal playing behind them.

Beyond this impressive front three, and left wing-back Mauricio Isla (who plays for Juventus), much of Chile's team play their club football in quite moderate environments. Influential centre-back Gary Medel was relegated to the English Championship with Cardiff prior to the World Cup. His team-mate Gonzalo Jara played in the Championship before the tournament too. Deep-lying midfielder Marcelo Diaz plays in Switzerland with FC Basel, Silva with Osasuna in Spain, and goalkeeper Claudio Bravo – at the age of 31 – was signed by Barcelona mid-tournament with question marks over whether he would play regular football at the Catalan giants. The rest of the team play their football in South America.

If Chile did not have a squad full of household names, they had the single most important thing that would made them a real force in Brazil – a tactical blueprint – *their* blueprint – that all the players evidently bought into, and opponents struggled to handle.

Chile's 3-4-3 v. Brazil

Chile's 3-4-3 formation in the knock-out stages of their game against hosts Brazil. Chile have developed an identity for playing with three centre-backs and playing aggressive football both in and out of possession.

Defying Their Identity

With a World Cup you should never take anything for granted. Teams that you would expect to possibly win the tournament – fail early on! After all Spain, Italy and England (although they were maybe not true contenders) all exited the competition in the group stages losing two of their three opening games. There are also those, like Costa Rica and the USA, who qualify for the tournament's knock-out stages, despite having been drawn in exceptionally difficult groups.

What you really do not expect to be writing about is how two nations with football entrenched in their psyche, and with a unique way of playing, can bend *so* much from their footballing identity. They did this however with winning, rather than sentiment in mind.

The Netherlands

It is hard to find a national footballing identity as strong at that found with the Netherlands. This identity is *so* fierce and *so* ingrained in the *Oranje* mindset that they have successfully exported it all over the world. Countless clubs and developing football countries, such as Ireland and Australia, have placed their national development programmes in the hands of Dutch coaches in an attempt to imitate the success of the Dutch coaching model, from youth through to professional football. We even find the legacy of the Dutch involvement in the Korean national team that has affected their national identity.

The quote at the start of the chapter from outspoken coach and fitness expert, Raymond Verheijen, shows just how much of an internal battle has raged in the Netherlands on the back of the 2014 World Cup. The Dutch public and media *expect* to see attractive football, seeped in the culture of *Total Football* that lit the world up in the 1970s under Rinus Michels. Their leading club, Ajax Amsterdam, also successfully implemented a system where technique and tactical fluency was, to them, the *only* way forward, and although the Godfather of Dutch football, Johan Cruyff, insists that winning is their first priority, one cannot help but feel that there is a national embarrassment to winning ugly – and many feel that winning is nothing without doing so in an entertaining manner.

The tactical approach of the Dutch at the 2014 World Cup was far removed from *The Dutch Way*. Not only did coach Louis van Gaal abandon his and the nation's trusted 4-3-3 formation in favour of a 3-4-1-2 (although not a system that is alien to the Dutch), he also chose to play a significant amount of this tournament *without the ball*. Staggeringly, only minnows Iran (29.7%) had less total possession than The Netherlands (39.5%) after their opening three groups games. Overall, The Netherlands were a lowly 20th when it came to overall possession at the 2014 World Cup (48.5%).

Instead of dominating possession, as is the *Oranje* trademark, they defended resolutely, pressed hard in midfield, and looked to hit their opponents with quick counter-attacks to allow their front pairing of Arjen Robben and Robin van Persie, with the assistance of Wesley Sneijder, to do their damage offensively. For van Gaal it was no longer about the Dutch being the flamboyant under-achievers (which has in itself almost become a footballing trait of the Dutch) – it was purely about winning.

Louis van Gaal's Favoured Attacking 4-3-3 (2-3-2-3)

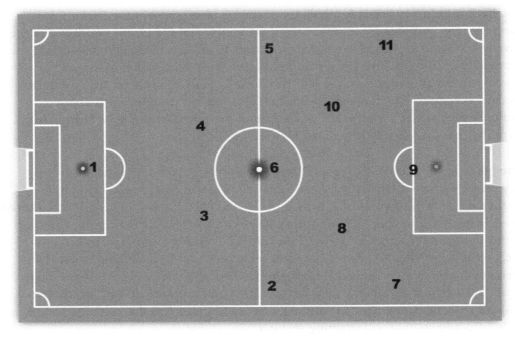

This 4-3-3, or 2-3-2-3 is van Gaal's favoured system from the Philosophy Vision document he produced during his time at Barcelona. Its attacking intent is clear from the advanced start positions of the players (e.g. full-backs over the half-way line).

Brazil

When you think of Brazil culturally, you think of colour, carnival, and smiles. When you think of Brazilian football, you think of wonderfully technical players, beach footballers from the favelas who could make fools of the best foreign players with their trickery, and a country that is passionate about their status at entertainers in world football. Consequently, when you think of Brazil at World Cup Finals, you think of flair, individuality, and a game firmly rooted in their flamboyant culture.

The Brazil we witnessed at their own World Cup however was far from that. They seemed rather more English in their set-up, although such a statement would probably never see me allowed to land in Rio or dare enter the Maracanã.

Like van Gaal, Luis Felipe Scolari, chose the pursuit of 'winning' football over 'Brazilian' football – he chose function over flamboyance. Two holding midfield players were a constant, with Wolfsburg's Luis Gustavo the main midfield destroyer, coupled with midfield workhorses, Paulinho, Fernandinho or occasionally Ramires. Against Mexico, attacking midfielder Oscar completed the most tackles in one game at the World Cup, with eight.

There is a legitimate suggestion that the team was built around Neymar, the so-called "golden boy" of the 2014 World Cup, with target strikers like Fred, and his usual replacement, Jo, designed to play high up against opposition centre-backs to allow Neymar more space to operate. You could be forgiven for assuming that the tactics were to allow Neymar to be the match-winner, and the others were there as the support-cast.

It was very common to see goalkeeper Julio Cesar choose to play longer, more direct passes to Fred / Jo, appearing less comfortable in taking calculated risks by building possession from the back. Prior to their last 16 encounter with Chile, word from the Brazilian camp was that they were seeking to use their height and physical advantage from set-plays as one of their main ploys to win the game – something you may be expected to hear from a functional mid-table English coach rather than a Brazilian World Cup winner! Their over-physical tactic of targeting Columbia's James Rodriguez in their quarter-final match was a tragic cultural shift from when their very own Pelé was kicked around World Cup pitches decades before that.

Pass, Take-on and Discipline Stats – Comparison of Final Four

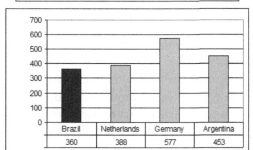

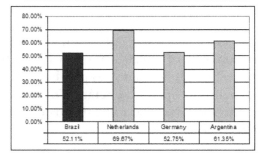

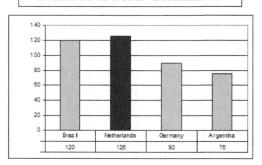

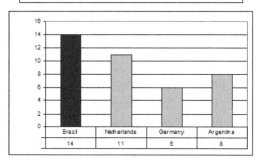

Evolving Football Cultures

Not all countries will have a unique, pinned-down football culture or national identity. Some national teams will change their approach frequently depending on the philosophy and style of their coach. Others will dabble in various tactics and styles, trying to find *their* optimal way of playing the beautiful game, either because they need an evolution to take them to the next level, or a revolution to take them back to the level they expect.

South Korea

The introduction of South Korean football to the world stage began in their enthralling campaign when they co-hosted the first ever Asian World Cup in 2002. Marshalled by Dutch coach Guus Hiddink, the South Koreans won the hearts of the world with their journey to the semi-finals, before eventually being knocked out by Germany.

The one thing you expect from the South Koreans is a work-ethic and physical conditioning that reflects the honesty that people stereotypically associate with this particular Asian culture; added to which one can add a well-honed football technique. Hiddink provided a Dutch-like structure and set of tactics to this work ethic and technical ability that brought such national delight and pride to the Korean fans and media. The Dutch influence would see attractive, possession-based football brought to the fore.

The 2014 reign of coach Hong Myung-Bo saw an attempted return to this Dutch focus, following a spell under Choi Kang-Hee where a forceful direct-style was preferred. Whether purists in the Netherlands would approve of the comparison is doubtful as although midfielder Ki Sung-Yueng had completed 100% of his passes by half-time of their opening game against Russia[2], the Koreans had played a number of wasteful, ill-judged longer passes, in particular to left-sided player, Son Heung-Min.

It may be more accurate to describe Myung-Bo's efforts to mix the Dutch influence with the more direct style of his predecessor, and accommodate the quick, counter-attacking play prized in Korea, as an attempt to mix the best of all worlds. Their youthful squad however will look to build on this having exited at the group stages, and a future without the guidance of Myung-Bo.

_____

[2] See below a breakdown of Ki's passing statistics from the 2014 World Cup. Note how his success rate is 100% when playing backwards or sideways, but fall when we study his attempted forward passes. Forward passes are always the most difficult as they involve taking more risks to create a goal.

Midfielder Ki Sung-Yueng Possession Statistics

Type of Pass	Successful / Attempted	Percentage Success
Group Game 1 v. Russia		
All Passes	65 / 69	94%
Forward	26 /30	87%
Square	18 / 18	100%
Backwards	21 / 21	100%
Group Game 2 v. Algeria		
All Passes	53 / 55	96%
Forward	23 / 25	92%
Square	14 / 14	100%
Backwards	16 / 16	100%
Group Game 3 v. Belgium		
All Passes	55 / 61	90%
Forward	37 / 43	86%
Square	10 / 10	100%
Backwards	8 / 8	100%

England

Much work has gone into England's footballing identity or "DNA" over the last decade or so. Due to the perceived lack of success at major tournaments since their only World Cup triumph at Wembley in 1966, a lot of soul-searching has been undertaken. The usual conclusions are always presented by supporters and the media following tournament exits – players are not technically good enough compared to their international rivals, youth coaching is based on brawn rather than brain, and tactically, English players simply do not understand the game well enough.

Traditionally, English teams were based around a direct-style 4-4-2 with a physically big centre-forward like Peter Crouch or Emile Heskey. Their game was about getting the ball forward quickly. This pace of play and directness can result in a lack of assured possession when asked to be patient with the ball or if asked to cut open a team who were defending resolutely. When asked to play in tight areas, the English traditionally favoured going over and around opposition bodies, rather than having the craft and guile to slice through them.

At the 2010 World Cup, the England coach Fabio Capello, tried to address difficulties around possession, and chose the smaller, more natural striker Jermain Defoe. The tactical limitations of Capello's 4-4-2 (or 4-4-1-1) was highlighted in the tournament, particularly when trying to deal with Germany's adventurous style and interchanging positions (something the Germans would go on to perfect in 2014).

Bizarrely, upon their win-less group-stage exit from the 2014 World Cup, the England team received arguably *less* criticism than they did when they were eliminated from the latter stages of previous tournaments against footballing powerhouses like Brazil and Germany. There was recognition that, although short-term gains were few, the long-term evolution of the team's style of play was moving in the right direction.

Head coach, Roy Hodgson, chose to field a 4-2-3-1 formation, largely based around players from Liverpool who had recently excelled playing a very brave, possession-based style – although it was never in Hodgson's own DNA to be as flamboyant as Liverpool boss Brendan Rodgers. As well as experienced international players like Steven Gerrard and Wayne Rooney, the English line-up had been freshened up with the inclusion of young, quick, exciting and almost unknown quantities like Adam Lallana (although 26 years old), Raheem Sterling and Daniel Sturridge – with others like Ross Barkley, Alex Oxlade-Chamberlain and Luke Shaw waiting in the wings (with Shaw's appearance in the final group game against Costa Rica, he became the youngest participant at the 2014 World Cup, at 18 years of age). In fact, 12 of their World Cup squad had less than 15 caps at the beginning of the tournament. There is a sense that England, in coming tournaments, may evolve and revolve around these gifted technicians, rather than around the big, powerful target strikers.

England's 4-2-3-1 v. Italy 2014

England used a 4-2-3-1 throughout their three games at the 2014 World Cup, unlike the 4-4-2 traditionally favoured by them.

England's Traditional 4-4-2 v Germany 2010 World Cup

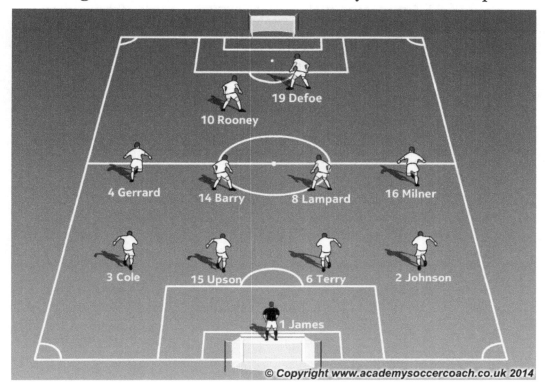

An example of the problematic 4-4-2 formation used by England. Its limitations were cruelly exposed by Germany in South Africa in 2010.

Summary

- Lots of national teams have their own, unique national footballing identity.
- During the 2014 World Cup, some teams adhered to this identity, others moved away from theirs completely, while others were seeking evolution or revolution in their playing style.
- Spain stuck to their tiki-taka style, but with limited success.
- Chile stuck to their fast-tempo philosophy, both in and out of possession.
- The Netherlands were happy to play a 3-4-1-2 style and forgo dominating possession, rather than stick to their *Total Football* roots.

- The South Koreans effectively aimed to mix the Dutch influence into their game, with fast counter-attacks, and the more direct style of their recent World Cup qualifying team.
- England moved away from the traditional 4-4-2 they become renowned for, using younger, more technical players in a 4-2-3-1.

2

Systems, Players, and Opponents

"The first task is to get to know the players really well – watching them as individuals in training and in match play to see what is good in their natural game. Then, and only then, can we begin to outline the general tactics." (Helenio Herrera, former Argentine coach of Inter Milan)

Thoroughbred believers in football tactics will feel that tactics alone can win games. Others believe in the spontaneity of football and that anything can happen which a game plan cannot predict or control. A particular strategy can go out the window with a goal, sending-off, poor refereeing decision, or a host of other incidents. Look at minnows Iran against giants Argentina. The Iranian tactic to defend deep was only undone by a typically magical moment from Lionel Messi. Do we judge their game plan then as having failed? Or was it successful and just needed that Messi strike to flash the other side of the upright? Let's face it, Iran may have even been 1-0 up had the referee given a foul by Pablo Zabaleta on Ashkan Dejagah and their game tactics would have been immortalised in the football history books.

Tactics can also be situational, as are team formations. How often do we hear commentators mention a forward player dropping deep to gain possession as he is not active enough in the game? Or teams going from all-out-attack to all-out-defence once they have scored? With all these puzzles in mind, let's look at the broad ways in which coaches select their teams, formations, and tactics.

The System, The Players, or The Opposition?

Hundreds of newspaper columns and online blogs will spend the days leading up to games trying to predict a team's starting line-line. Games will be previewed and predictions made about their outcomes based on the players selected. One of the most intriguing questions posed of a coach, then, is how to choose his team. Does he identify a system to play, and chose the players to fit that system? Does he select the 'best' players and mould a system around them? And what impact does the opposition have on this process? Of course there will also be countless other situational decisions – what injuries the team is carrying, what players are in form or not, and what is riding on the match.

Fitting Players into The System

With a World Cup squad of 23 players, the easy thing to do would be to pick two players for each position (with three goalkeepers). This may have been quite a rational thing to do say 20 years ago, but in modern football, this is far too rigid to be effective.

A coach who sticks steadfastly to a particular formation or system would feel far more comfortable in doing this than one who changes his players or formation as events unfold. Argentina, for example, began their first group game playing a 3-5-1-1 formation but Alejandro Sabella, their coach, abandoned it at half-time and never returned to it. The Argentines spent the rest of the tournament moving between a 4-3-3, 4-4-2, 4-2-3-1 and, depending on the circumstances of the game, a containing, defensive 4-5-1.

Picking a squad with two expert players in each position is not, however, an exact science, nor should it be. Normally several squad players who can play at least two positions are included to allow extra space in any squad for the inclusion of impact players who may offer something different and may assist in a change of formation or focus. In 2006, for example, Germany included speedy, uncapped midfielder David Odonkor is the squad, and used the player's ability to run 100 metres in under 11 seconds as a weapon from the substitutes' bench.

At the 2014 World Cup Didier Deschamps had a selection decision to make over which of his two Premier League full-backs to opt for as starting full-back – Mathieu Debuchy of mid-table Newcastle United[1] or Bacary Sagna who had just secured a bumper contract at champions Manchester City having left Champions League side Arsenal. One would assume that Sagna would be favourite for this slot, but instead Deschamps opted for Debuchy as he felt he was the more dynamic, forward-thinking of the two.

Belgium

Much has been made of Belgium's recent meteoric rise in terms of talent development. Their whole development process is based around a 4-2-3-1 formation (or variants of it) and has produced a generation of world-class players like Vincent Kompany, Thibaut Courtois, Eden Hazard, and Romelu Lukaku, amongst others.

The one positional area that remains a problem for the current Belgian side is in the full-back positions. Of the eight defenders named in their World Cup squad, only one was a natural full-back in the shape of right-back Anthony Vanden Borre (who incidentally only played in Belgium's final group game against South Korea when their path into the knock-out stages was already secure).

Belgium's steadfast stance around playing with a back four, rather than playing in an arguably more suitable back three, saw centre-backs Toby Alderweireld at right-back and either Jan Vertonghen or Thomas Vermaelen at left-back.

This may be a reason why team tactics in Brazil were was to play in a more direct style from the goalkeeper, rather than risking possession by playing through the full-backs (although, being modern centre-backs, they are very good technicians). Considering the abundance of excellent attacking midfield players Belgium possess in Eden Hazard, Kevin De Bruyne, Nacer Chadli, Adnan Januzaj, Dries Mertens and Kevin Mirallas (plus Marouane Fellaini who played their 'dead rubber' game against the Koreans in the central attacking midfield position), starting with three of the six may well be the natural option – something they consistently altered along with their main striker.

---

[1] Ironically Debuchy has been signed by Arsenal as Sagna's replacement.

Game Time (Minutes) of Belgium's Attacking Players

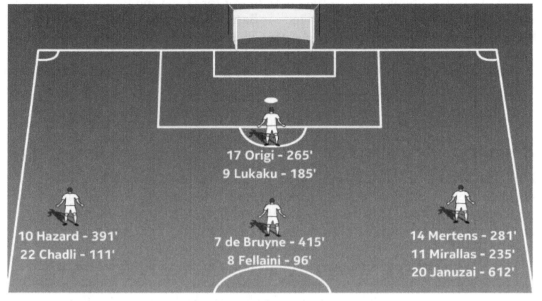

17 Origi - 265'
9 Lukaku - 185'

10 Hazard - 391'
22 Chadli - 111'

7 de Bruyne - 415'
8 Fellaini - 96'

14 Mertens - 281'
11 Mirallas - 235'
20 Januzai - 612'

Hazard and De Bruyne were the most certain of their places in Belgium's attacking midfield positions, but in total seven players were used across the attacking midfield three positions. Lukaku and Divock Origi essentially shared the number 9 role, although Mirallas also featured there briefly.

Russia

Also in Belgium's group was Fabio Capello's Russia. The Italian coach favoured setting his team up in a 4-3-3 in the opening game, before changing to a 4-2-3-1 subsequently. In their opener against South Korea, the former England World Cup coach picked his players around his system, choosing the youthful Aleksandr Kokorin ahead of experienced forward Aleksandr Kerzhakov, rather than finding a way of including both (incidentally he did include both in their must-win final group game against Algeria). Before the World Cup many believed that Kokorin would instead play from the left in an effort to get both threatening players into the starting 11.

In addition to the exclusion of Kerzhakov, Capello also left creative attacking midfielder Alan Dzagoev out of the team. The Italian, who favoured a team built on solid defensive foundations, rather than an open, attacking one (that was common at the 2014 World Cup) felt Dzagoev did not work hard enough within his system, and was happy to forgo using the midfielder's dribbling skills and ability to change games with something different in the attacking third. Interestingly, when 1-0 down to the

Koreans, with both Kerzakov and Dzagoev on as substitutes, Russia developed a much greater attacking threat, looking more incisive and willing to take risks in an effort to equalise, which they did through substitute Kerzhakov.

England and France

Going into the tournament, there were several question marks over the team England's Roy Hodgson would pick in his preferred 4-2-3-1 formation. There were no question marks at all, however, as to whether the former Switzerland World Cup coach would deviate from this system.

The main question was about the deployment of key striker, Wayne Rooney. Given the rise to prominence of Daniel Sturridge, whose 18 months as a central attacker at Liverpool made him the obvious choice to start as the number nine, Rooney was tipped to move either to the left side or play as the number 10.

It was clear Hodgson wanted both in the team, as they were the country's two best match-winners, but by playing Rooney in attacking midfield positions, rather than in a preferred central striker role he was clearly choosing his players ahead of his system. This can be compared and contrasted to France's use of their 4-3-3 formation, in particular in their second group game against neighbours Switzerland.

To get both Olivier Giroud and Karim Benzema into the team, the latter, like Rooney, was moved from his role as main striker to the left hand side. Interestingly, however, France coach Didier Deschamps adapted the role to suit the Real Madrid man by using his central midfield players, notably Blaise Matuidi, to track attack-minded Swiss full-back Stephan Lichtsteiner, rather than force Benzema to defend in his own half. This was a deliberate ploy to allow France to counter-attack in the space left behind (we will take a closer look at this tactic in a later chapter). Rooney, when used on the left, on the other hand, was expected to do this defensive work which often left England vulnerable down their left hand side against Italy's dynamic right-back Matteo Darmian.

The Rooney – Darmian Duel

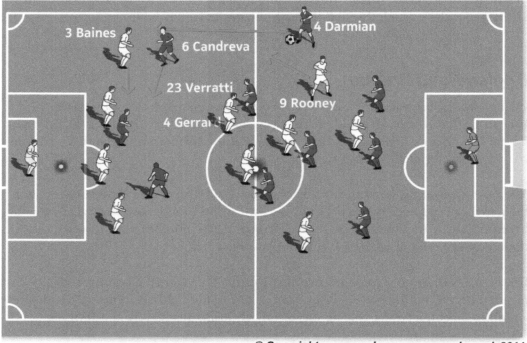

With Rooney playing out of position, on the left, he struggled to contain the forward-thinking Italian right full-back Darmian. Those who could offer cover were also occupied. Gerrard was occupied by compact Italian midfielders (in this case Marco Verratti) and left-back Leighton Baines by the runs of Antonio Candreva from wide right into central positions.

The Players Choose the System

Lots of coaches are deeply entrenched in playing 'their' system. They will therefore choose players that fit said system, or decide whether a player can play the system, even if it is not quite a square peg in a square hole. Other coaches, however, turn this on its head, almost refusing to play players 'out of position' or in an unfamiliar area to them. Their team and squad selection therefore will be based around the team's most effective players, and the rest of the team will be set up to allow the key players to flourish.

This, of course, like anything in football, is not an exact science. Germany could not possibly include all their skilful attacking players – partly because they almost have too many of them! André Schürrle, for example, was mostly used from the substitutes' bench, while Julian Draxler completed a mere handful of minutes at the World Cup – and we must remember that Marco Reus suffered a tournament-ending injury in the days leading up to the World Cup. Germany could not possibly include them all, but Löw's fluid attacking system allowed him to include as many as he could.

Argentina

During their opening game of the World Cup, the Argentina coach, Sabella, surprised all of us by playing with three central defenders, moving away from the typical 4-3-3 that the team had usually preferred. The idea behind using this formation allowed him to play the talented trio of Sergio Agüero, Lionel Messi and Angel di Maria, in central areas.

This opening game, against Bosnia, did not go especially well for Sabella's side and the 3-5-1-1 was abandoned at half-time in favour of their more favoured 4-3-3. For the second half Argentina reverted to a back 4, and added Napoli striker Gonzalo Higuaín to partner Agüero up front, which allowed Messi to drop off into more of a free role between the midfield and strikers. Sabella, in an effort to balance his side now playing with three strikers and di Maria as an attacking midfielder, introduced Fernando Gago to help fellow midfielder Javier Mascherano give the team some defensive protection. This balance between choosing his best attacking options, and balancing the team defensively saw Argentina progress to the final. It was only the last seven minutes of extra-time in the final against Germany that Argentina fell behind at any point in the tournament.

After the opening game Argentina's starting formation was criticised publicly by captain Messi, who claimed he and fellow striker Agüero felt isolated and "suffered" during the first half playing 3-5-1-1. Prior to Argentina's second game against Iran, Sabella open-mindedly responded: "We can all make mistakes you know. Tomorrow we will start with a 4-3-3 formation and we will take it from there. We may have to change the formation or not." (via FIFA.com).

Sabella's stance towards tactics and formations, and his willingness to change them if necessary was evident throughout the tournament. This was usually based on the best attacking options he felt he had open to him. Higuaín became the mainstay of the Argentine forward-line, with Messi and di Maria also certain starters throughout the tournament. Having lost Agüero to injury against Nigeria, Ezequiel Lavezzi came into the side, which prompted another change in Argentine formation, utilising either a 4-2-3-1 or 4-4-2 for the remainder of the competition.

Argentina's Changeable Tactics

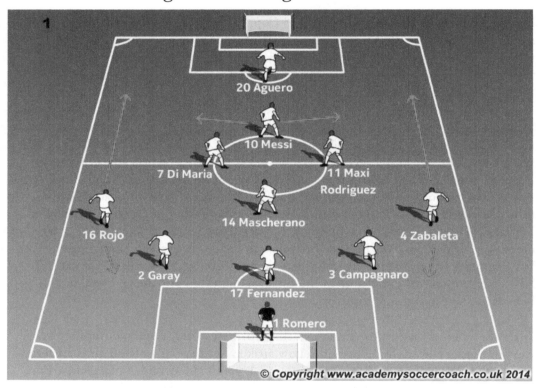

1. Argentina's 3-5-1-1 from the first half of their opening game v. Bosnia

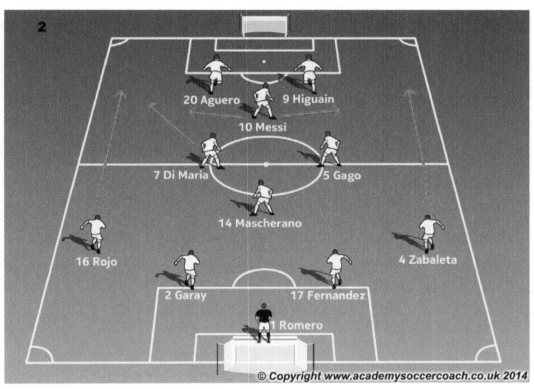

2. Reverting to 4-3-3 in second game v. Iran in reaction to criticism of 3-5-1-1

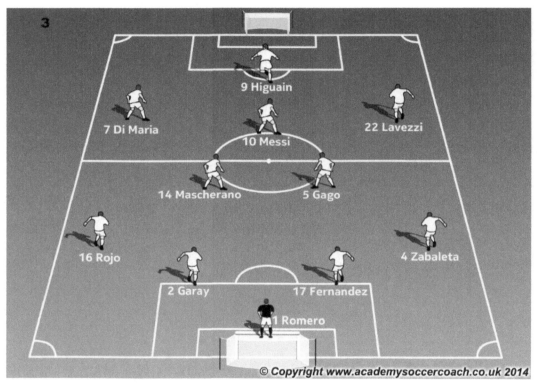

3. Argentina's change of shape to 4-2-3-1 with Lavezzi replacing the injured Agüero against Switzerland

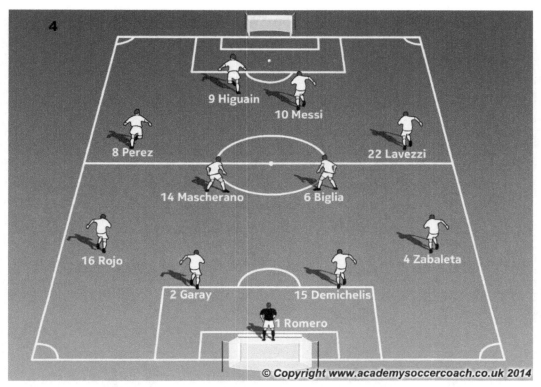

4. The 4-3-2-1 evolving to a more traditional 4-4-2 with the loss of Di Maria in the World Cup Final v. Germany

Sabella will feel quite justified regarding his selection policy at the 2014 World Cup. Messi of course was the star of their side, and was the winner (although controversially according to some2) of the Golden Ball – the World Cup's best player. Trademark Messi goals against Bosnia and Iran, added to his brace against Nigeria, saw Argentina safely into the knock-out phase of the tournament. Although di Maria had a poor game against Switzerland, he scored the winning goal in extra-time to take Argentina into the quarter-finals, and Higuaín's expertly taken goal against Belgium and influence as a substitute in the Bosnia match, showed that Sabella's insistence on match-winners and a defensive balance proved decisive on numerous occasions.

———————————

2 Interestingly, although opinion varied, Messi received the highest individual score on whoscored.com, a website that translates performances into a tangible score out of 10 based on certain actions and calculations during games. See the Team of the Tournament from whoscored.com based on these ratings below.

www.whoscored.com World Cup Best XI

The Netherlands

Most surprisingly, one of the coaches who chose his system to best suit his players was Netherlands coach, Louis van Gaal. The Dutchman had always been steadfast around his use of a 4-3-3 formation. Quoted in an interview, early in 2014, van Gaal said: "I'm always going back to the vision, then the team, and then which players fit in my system, a 1-4-3-3, because I'm always playing that."

Those of you who have seen van Gaal's playing philosophy document during his time at Barcelona (available online) will know that the Dutchman bases his playing style around the team and happily foregoes the role of the individual. He has famously fallen out with countless star players across his time in coaching when they did not adhere to 'his' system.

The blueprint for the Netherlands' tactics in Brazil however was thrown into chaos with the injury of key midfielder Kevin Strootman two months before the start of the tournament.

Rather than persist with his favoured 4-3-3 in light of his midfield man's absence, van Gaal altered his approach and set his team out in a 3-4-3 instead. This gave the tactically meticulous coach only a matter of weeks to prepare his team around this new layout.

Strootman's absence was not the only consideration for the Dutch. Adding a third centre-back allowed attack-orientated wing-backs, particularly Danny Blind, greater defensive protection. It also allowed them to utilise their best front three players of Robben, van Persie and Wesley Sneijder - all tied together with the combative and straightforward central midfielders, Nigel de Jong and Jonathan de Guzman.

Netherlands 3-4-3 Line-Up v. Spain

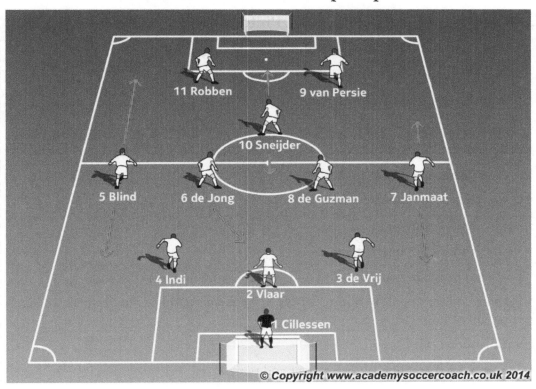

Chapter 2

Changing Tactics for Specific Opponents

Lots of coaches can battle with team selection at the best of times. Above we see that some will be steadfast around a formation, and fit players into it, whilst others will choose their key players and revolve their formation and tactics around these players.

An important consideration, however, is also the opposition, something coaches doubtlessly consider. Often the coaches of top international teams will stick with *their* plan, worrying more about themselves and doing *their* job correctly, rather than focusing on the opposition. Below, for example, is a hand-out from a team briefing from Arséne Wenger and Arsenal in preparation for an away fixture at Bolton Wanderers. Note Arsenal's insistence on "our identity" away from home as well as at home.

Arsenal Philosophy

Our team becomes stronger by:

• Display a positive attitude on and off the pitch

• Everyone making the right decisions for the team

• Have an unshakeable belief that we can achieve our target

• Believe in the strength of the team

• Always want more – always give more

• Focus on our communication

• Be demanding with yourself

• Be fresh and well prepared to win

• Focus on being mentally stronger and always keep going until the end

• When we play away from home, believe in *our identity* and play the football we love to play at home

• Stick together

• Stay grounded and humble as a player and person

• Show the desire to win in all that you do

• Enjoy and contribute to all that is special about being in a team – don't take it for granted

Algeria

The Algerians surprised and impressed lots of people in Brazil, and their four games in the 2014 World Cup provide us with a great case study on tactical changeability. Their ability to drastically change tack, literally from game to game, was arguably their most impressive attribute. This nous allowed them to qualify from Group H ahead of Russia and they gleaned more praise from their four point haul then group rivals Belgium who topped the group with nine points from the nine available.

Defend Deep v. Belgium

It was against the Belgians that Algeria's campaign started. Their distinct game plan was to morph their 4-2-3-1 formation into a 4-5-1 when out of possession, with the aim of containing Belgium and hitting them with quick counter-attacks. Having gone ahead after 25 minutes with a well taken penalty from Sofiane Feghouli, following a fast-flowing move which caught out Belgium's make-shift left-back Jan Vertonghen, their game plan was coming into effect nicely. Belgian coach Marc Wilmots was less impressed calling the Algerians "a team that refused to play football". While this sort of statement is a common slight from high level coaches when struggling to break down dogged, underdog defences, Wilmots' point was backed up by Algeria's comfort in playing the game without the ball, achieving only 32.1% of possession (only slightly less than they had over 120 minutes against eventual champions Germany) – and managing only three attempts on goal.

Wilmots was forced into changing his line-up at the break, as, even with the wealth of talent in the Belgian side, they did not look to have the creative edge to open up Algeria's stubborn defensive set-up and were restricted mainly to shots from distance. It was two substitutes that were to drag Belgium to victory.

When a team is defending deep, coaches often look for creative players to prise teams open with something special (as Eden Hazard did for Belgium with a deliberate run and assist against Russia), try to go around the 'block' of defenders and look for crosses, or play directly and look to go over the block. On 70 minutes, Belgium did just that with a De Bruyne cross finding the head of Marouane Fellaini, who expertly glanced in the equaliser. Using Fellaini's height as a tactic became a much-used weapon for Belgium in subsequent games. Against Russia, the joint highest number of pass combinations (11) was from goalkeeper Courtois to Fellaini positioned in an advanced area. According to FIFA statistics, Fellaini's average position against the Russians was more advanced than their number '10' Kevin De Bruyne.

Belgium Average Positions v. Russia

*Having made an impact as a substitute against Algeria, Fellaini went from substitute to starter against Russia. The tactic of going long and high into the midfielder, especially from goalkeeper Courtois, saw this tactic affect the average position of the Belgian side, with Fellaini's average position further forward than number '10' De Bruyne. *Jan Vertonghen replaced starter Thomas Vermaelen after 30 minutes.*

If Algeria felt hurt that all their good defensive work was undone with a headed goal from a cross, their manner in ultimately losing the game will give them nightmares. Having regained possession in their defensive third, Belgium's villain-cum-hero Vertonghen managed to cut open the Algerians with just one pass to set Hazard away and Belgium with a 3v2 advantage, bearing down on Raïs M'Bolhi's goal. His pass and the subsequent finish from Dries Mertens saw Algeria ultimately beaten at their own game – punished severely with a swift counter-attack from deep.

All Out Attack v. South Korea

If a solid Algerian defensive performance impressed everyone outside of Algeria (the national media insisted with some justification that the squad had players who were built to attack), their approach to their second game against South Korea was to amaze even further.

This was a footballing Jekyll and Hyde without the connotations of crazy. Their approach seemed as if they knew that a victory was a must against, on paper, their weakest opponent in the group. Algeria raced into a three-goal lead before half-time, their third goal a version of incisive, inventive tiki-taka football that the Spanish or Germans would have been rightly proud of.

The openness of the game was only going to result in more goals, and South Korea did manage to get on the scoresheet twice, either side of a Yacine Brahimi goal to see the game finish 4-2 to the Algerians. A third game-plan was now needed to achieve at least a draw against stuttering Russian opponents and send the Africans into the World Cup knock-out rounds for the first time in their history.

Clever and Combative v. Russia

Their third group game against Russia threw up one of those great knock-out competition conundrums. A draw would take Algeria through, whereas the Russian giants needed to win. With this in mind, it was Capello's side who naturally set about dominating the early stages of the game, and scoring after only six minutes through striker Kokorin.

A combative Algerian performance followed, understanding their need to score, but also that patience was required, to ensure they did not fall even further behind. Eventually Algeria did equalise through Islam Sliming after an hour, heading in from a wide free-kick, although the goal is as much remembered for a laser beam being shone in the eyes of Russian goalkeeper Igor Akinfeev. The equaliser allowed Algeria the opportunity to revert to their Belgian template and defend resolutely. From an Algerian point of view, they were thankful Russia did not possess a Fellaini of their own and they managed hold onto a point to take them through to a meeting with the much-fancied Germans.

Quality and Lack of Quality v. Germany

Outsiders looked at this game as one of high predictability – a David versus Goliath battle that would be won comfortably by the Europeans. When the curtain closed on this Round of 16 game, it was indeed the possession-based Goliath who was victorious – but the counter-attacking David gave him a real scare.

Of Germany's six opponents on their path to the World Cup Final, it was Algeria who made them look as vulnerable as any. The Africans were left to rue a number of good chances through both the brilliance of German stopper Manuel Neuer and their own wastefulness in front of goal. Had they have been capable of taking those chances, the 2014 World Cup would have had a different name engraved on the Jules Rimet trophy.

It was another game that was again famous for Algeria's opposition goalkeeper. With Algeria counter-attacking consistently, especially in the first half, German goalkeeper Neuer was frequently called into action to sweep up Algerian encroachments beyond his back four. He took a total of 17 touches outside his penalty box – a record number for a goalkeeper – and redefined the 'sweeper-keeper' tag.

As the game progressed, and with Germany proving to be the masters of ball retention, the Algerians grew tired and their adventures into German territory became less and less frequent. Later in the book we will examine the trend where teams who play a counter-attacking tactic end up with less of the possession, but more of the clear-cut chances (ultimately though, the longer the game goes on, the fewer chances these counter-attacks produce). Algeria were left to rue some glorious chances, especially in the first half, and three goals in extra-time saw them defeated 2-1 and knocked out of the competition.

On paper, one win from four games might not herald a lot of praise for tactical nous, but Algeria certainly left their adaptable tactical mark on the 2014 World Cup.

Manuel Neuer Touches Outside the Box v. Algeria

Graphic of Manuel Neuer's 17 touches outside of the box against Algeria.

Summary

- Tactics are situational and can be affected by moments in the game.
- Belgium and England chose their players to fit into their 4-2-3-1 system.
- The Russian national team sacrificed the use of a strike partnership by selecting Kokorin as a lone forward, rather than using both him and Kerzhakov, except in their final game when they needed to win.
- England and France both used strikers in wide left positions, but used them differently.
- Germany, the Netherlands and Argentina both found ways of including their best players in their starting line-up, adapting their formation and tactics around these players.
- In terms of altering tactics to cater for the opposition, Algeria did so most frequently and most dramatically.

3
With Back Fours

"The problem with this 4-2-3-1 is that it very quickly becomes a 4-4-2 or at least a 4-4-1-1 and we end up with flat lines and people getting between us" (Gary Lineker, former England International on England's 4-2-3-1)

The 2014 World Cup in Brazil gave us lots of variation in terms of team formations. We saw teams play with a traditional back four, those that played with three central defenders and wing-backs, and teams that played with a back five. Cameroon spent most of their encounter against Mexico essentially playing with a back six, though I'm certain this was a consequence of how the game unfolded, rather than a specific tactical ploy.

We saw teams that played with one and two holding central midfield players, use a midfield diamond, play with two wingers, one winger or no wingers at all – and while most teams used either one or two strikers, some played without a recognised centre-forward and, on occasions, teams used three out-and-out strikers.

Of the four semi-finalists, we saw Holland mainly play a 3-4-3, Germany mainly a 4-3-3 but using a 'false 9', Brazil used a 4-2-3-1 and Argentina rotated significantly from 3-5-1-1, to 4-4-2, a 4-4-1-1 and 4-2-3-1. Colombia, one of the surprise packages and entertainers of the World Cup (although with a FIFA rank of fourth before the competition), played a 4-4-2 which morphed into a 4-2-2-2 against Uruguay.

Fluidity

Before we get stuck into an analysis of the back four formations at the 2014 World Cup, let's just pause and acknowledge something mentioned in the introductory chapter around the "numbers game". Below, we have used *typical* formation numbers in a bid to give an indication into the shape of teams on the field of play.

The truth is that team shapes and formations are becoming more and more fluid, and are therefore getting more difficult to analyse using formation numbers alone, so we will look at some of the interesting tactical set-ups, using formations as our starting point.

Furthermore, as we will discuss in more detail later in the book, players no longer simply stick to one 'position'. Full-backs burst forward, centre-backs carry the ball into the opposition half, midfielders rotate, attacking midfield players seem to play anywhere they are needed, and strikers now have responsibilities that are about more than just scoring goals. So while we use Germany as an example of a 4-3-3, amongst the free-flowing nature of a live game, their 'numbers' can virtually be ripped apart. The numbers are (at best) starting positions, as we will see.

Four-Two-Three-One – Popularity and Decline

Fluidity within 4-2-3-1 systems can vary. In Brazil, we saw teams use it to defend deep and counter-attack (Switzerland v. France), contain the opposition (Russia), dominate possession (Spain), play a direct style (Belgium) and attack in numbers (Germany). Below we will look at the fluidity of Germany in the context of their 4-3-3, but this remained similar when they utilised a 4-2-3-1 in the early stages of the competition. It is no coincidence that the most fluid team at the World Cup went on to become champions. Arguably, the technical ability and game understanding of individual German players (and as a group) won them the World Cup, regardless of formation.

Popularity

For the second World Cup running, 4-2-3-1 proved to be the most popular formation. Although lots of teams chose the 4-2-3-1, many of them had a different way of playing it. Brazil constantly rotated the position of their supporting midfield three with Oscar, Neymar, and Hulk mainly being selected in different positions for different games. The Belgians were similar although they used more players across these positions, including Eden Hazard, Kevin de Bruyne, Dries Mertens, Nacer

Chadli, Kevin Mirallas and Adnan Januzaj (all used at different points during Belgium's progression to the knock-out stages).

Colombia's use of 4-2-3-1 saw their attacking midfield three in more consistent positions. Golden boot winner James Rodriguez played centrally (mostly, but we will look at that later in the chapter), with winger Juan Guillermo Cuadrado used from the right, and Víctor Ibarbo from the left. On the brief occasions when Argentina used the system, Messi would be selected to play centrally (although with the freedom to roam) and allow Ángel Di María and Ezequiel Lavezzi the liberty to swap sides. The USA on the other hand seemed happier to use their advanced midfielders in set positions, with central players Jermaine Jones and Michael Bradley more box-to-box midfield players, rather than attackers in the guise of Neymar, de Bruyne, or Messi.

Decline

Although 4-2-3-1 was the default of the 2010 World Cup, and the most popular one again in Brazil, there appears to be a tactical evolution afoot that will see it superseded. After all, all styles and formations have their shelf life as people learn how to combat them. There is a real suggestion that the system appears to have become stale, particularly considering the tactical tinkerings of van Gaal, Sabella, Jorge Luis Pinto, et al.

Those who are critical of 4-2-3-1, like Gary Lineker in the opening quote of this chapter, will point to teams playing with a straight line of three behind one striker. As teams are so used to this now, it is very defendable for teams they play against. The central midfield pairing that plays as a *double pivot* can often become exposed in a way that 4-4-2 had before it went out of fashion. During the 2010 World Cup in South Africa, the double pivot was king. All four semi-finalists used it (although Uruguay used something akin to a 4-4-2 rather than the 4-2-3-1 of Spain, Holland and Germany). When pressed this midfield two can also be exposed, especially when up against a midfield three.

Indeed the similarities between 4-2-3-1 and out-of-favour 4-4-2 are noticeable, especially when out of possession. In an attempt to become compact, the attacking midfield three will drop into defensive positions, as the diagram below illustrates. The players that are most useful when playing in between lines, and away from defenders, have now created these lines and become the defenders.

Brazil Out of Possession Shape v. Croatia

Out of possession, 4-2-3-1 formations can become similar to a 4-4-2, with two banks of four and one of the forward players dropping in to help defensively. This screenshot was of Brazil's out of possession shape against Croatia.

Uruguay's Opening Goal v. England's 4-2-3-1

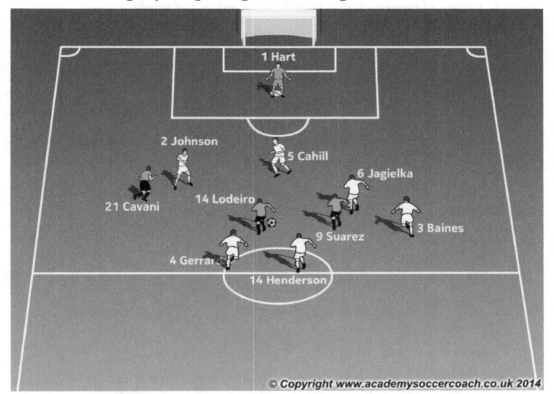

Uruguay's opening goal against England typified the disadvantages of having a flat two as the double pivot. Once Uruguay won possession and broke past Gerrard and Henderson, Uruguay could attack a disorganised back four, and although outnumbered 3v4 by the England defenders, the pace and precision of their attack could out-manoeuvre a disordered England back four.

Spot the Difference – Brazil v. Croatia

Day one of the World Cup saw Brazil and Croatia face-off and the battles of the 4-2-3-1 formations commence. Brazil, playing at home and riding the wave of fanaticism that had swept through the country, looked to dominate the ball and set the attacking tone. Although the Croatian coach, Niko Kovač, insisted he wouldn't "park the bus", a term used to indicate ultra-defensiveness, his team were set up to defend their own half and look for ways to counter-attack. The most outstanding difference in terms of player selection was less the attacking midfield three this time, but the style of players used in their midfield two.

Brazil opted for the power of Luis Gustavo and Paulinho and, later in the game, Ramires was brought into the team for his extra legs. In contrast, however, Group A rivals Croatia, famed for their small, yet technically impressive players, chose a midfield pairing of the diminutive Luka Modric and Ivan Rakitić.

Brazil's 4-2-3-1 v. Croatia 4-2-3-1

© Copyright www.academysoccercoach.co.uk 2014

Although Modric and Rakitić were Croatia's two most important and influential players, along with left-back Šime Vrsaljko, it was the Brazilian's power that was to be the deciding factor.

Haven taken the lead early in the game, though a quick counter-attack which saw Ivica Olić's left-wing cross turned into his own goal by the recovering Marcelo, Croatia then became even happier to defend deeply behind the halfway line and try to contain the Brazilians. Brazil received an early warning-shot about Croatia's quick counter-attacks when Olić again threatened their goal with a misplaced header. This tactic saw Brazil limited to chances arising mainly from set-pieces, with Croatia only pressing in Brazil's half if they felt they had the chance of winning the ball back, but otherwise allowing Brazil to pass the ball sideways or backwards.

Brazil's equaliser highlighted their midfield power, and was a sign of their focus on work-rate and tackling power in the central areas. It was Oscar on this occasion, whose vigour and determination saw him force a way through both Rakitić and Modric. The ball landed at the feet of Neymar who had taken up a position between Croatia's two deep-lying midfielders and centre-backs to strike home from distance.

It was Neymar who also added a second from the penalty-spot in the second-half, before Ramires was introduced for him in the closing stages, with Luis Felipe Scolari looking to add even more work-rate at the expense of their main flair player. It was this energy that saw Ramires capitalise on hesitation from Rakitić, powering him to the ground as he stole possession, allowing Oscar to run at the Croatian defence, and fire home a futsal-like, disguised shot from outside the box.

Although Brazil had dominated possession (62% to 38%), it was their decision to build power into their midfield, which was the deciding factor in winning the game.

Four-Three-Three

Although 4-2-3-1 was the most popular, there was a significant presence of teams that played with variations of a 4-3-3 formation.

From Russia with a Violin String

Russia began the tournament using quite a traditional 4-3-3, and the most conventional variant of it as we know it. Unlike the 4-2-3-1, they used just one holding midfielder, Denis Glushakov, with two midfielders ahead of him who would join in the attacks, and the use of two wide players in Yuri Zhirkov and Aleksandr Samedov.

What separates differing types of 4-3-3 formations is the use of the front three, and in particular the two wide players. Often teams will use "wrong-footed" (or inverted) wingers (for example, left-footed players from the right and vice versa). Sometimes they will employ a fluid, rotating three, and maybe even use two or three strikers. In their game against South Korea, after which coach Fabio Capello abandoned the system, Russia fielded the left-footed Zhirkov on the left and right-footed Samedov on the right, with quick, young striker Alexander Kokorin through the middle, hence my use of the term "traditional" in describing their approach.

Russia's 4-3-3 v. South Korea

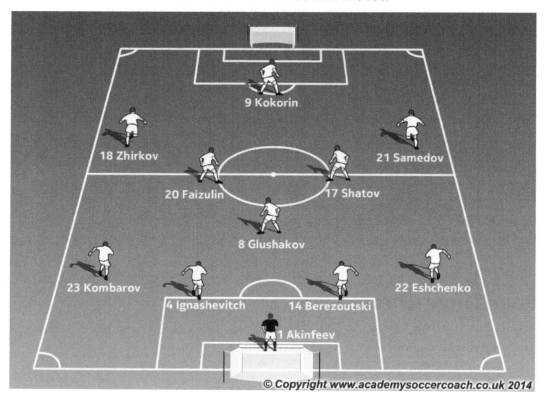

While many teams in the opening stages, especially footballing powerhouse nations, looked to attack and play an open game, the Russians were quite conservative. Even in the post-match analysis, Capello seemed content, as his team had "been as tight as a violin string". Their 4-3-3 often morphed into a 4-5-1 with Kokorin having very little to feed off as a lone striker. It took South Korea to take the lead before Capello introduced substitutes Kerzhakov and Dzagoev to add some attacking intent and ingenuity. The Russian performance, compared to other teams, almost threw us back to the trend of World Cup 2010, where avoiding defeat seemed more important than trying to win in the early games. When Russia did take risks, however, in the last 20 minutes, they looked dangerous, and left us wondering what impact they may have had at the World Cup had they taken more chances and played a more adventurous 4-3-3.

The French Connections

Like the Russians, France utilised a 4-3-3, but offered us more variation in how they did so. While Russia abandoned their system in favour of a 4-2-3-1 after their opening game, the French tweaked their system through the competition to accommodate two out-and-out strikers in their team.

After their two opening games, and in an effort to get both strikers Karim Benzema and Olivier Giroud into the side, French coach Didier Deschamps adjusted his tactical shape by rotating natural wide man Antoine Griezmann in and out of the team, replacing him with Giroud as the central striker, and utilising Karim Benzema from the left-hand side.

France 4-3-3 v. Switzerland

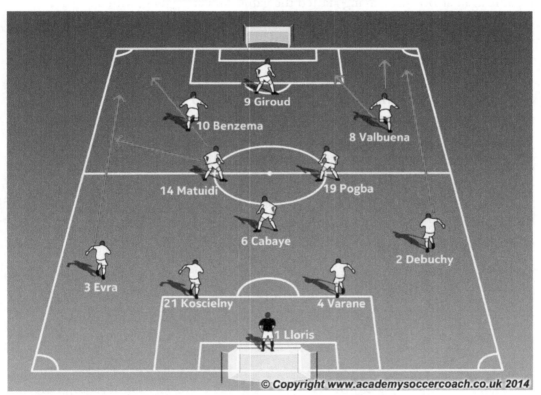

© Copyright www.academysoccercoach.co.uk 2014

Rather than expect Benzema, however, to completely adapt his game and play as an out-and-out winger, akin to Russia's Zhirkov, the Real Madrid striker (who ironically was one of only two strikers in the World Cup top 10 scoring charts with three goals despite being used a lot in this wide-left position) ventured inside to play closer to Giroud.

The balance of the rest of the team was important to address Benzema's role in the team. Key to this was how Deschamps utilised Blaise Matuidi, whose energy, left-footedness and experience as a wide player, allowed him to cover the spaces left by Benzema, both in possession, with the assistance of left-back Patrice Evra, and out of possession. We will look at Benzema's role in this position when out of possession at a later point in this book.

Argentina Do It Differently

If France's conundrum was about getting both strikers Benzema and Giroud into the starting line-up, Argentina faced a similar problem entering their opening Group F game against Bosnia. Having started the game, and struggling, with a 3-5-1-1 formation, coach Alejandro Sabella ripped up their half-time script, added Gonzalo Higuain and Fernando Gago, and changed to a 4-3-3.

Argentina's Second-Half 4-3-3 v. Bosnia

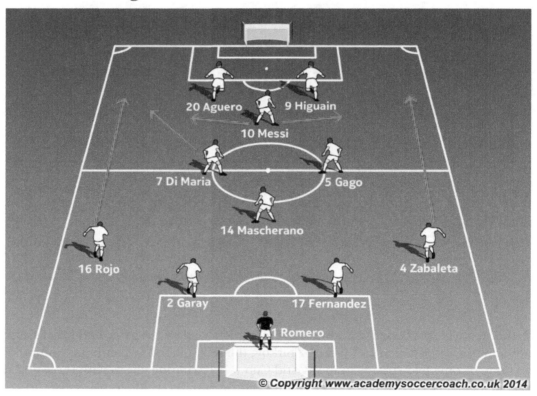

Rather than using one central striker, flanked by two support players, Argentina narrowed their midfield, played with two dangerous strikers in Agüero and Higuain, and supported by Lionel Messi from a deeper position. In the first half, Messi struggled to have an impact on the game, often picking the ball up in crowded midfield areas and having little room to manoeuvre. There were too many Eastern European bodies between him, the ball, and the Bosnian goal.

With the addition of a second striker, both Higuain and Agüero could occupy and push back the Bosnian back four, allowing Messi more room to operate and hurt them. This was typified by their goal, where Messi picked up possession deep and exchanged passes with Higuain, before expertly finishing in goalkeeper Asmir Begović's bottom right-hand corner.

The structure of the Argentine midfield was important to allow them to play with two strikers and a free-role for Messi. Angel Di Maria made Matuidi-like ventures to the left-hand side and a more disciplined Gago helped Mascherano protect the back four, further allowing the attacking ventures of full-backs Marcos Rojo and Pablo Zabaleta.

Germany's Organised Chaos

If Argentina's 4-3-3 style was innovative and played to their strengths, Germany offered us another, even more dynamic variation of it. It was a formation that allowed coach Joachim Löw the opportunity to include as many of his creative, diminutive attacking midfield players as he dared, plus utilise his ever-changing but dynamic full-backs. Having only brought 34-year-old Miroslav Klose to the World Cup as a recognised striker, Germany embarked on a campaign to win the biggest international competition accepting that they would play significant amounts of football striker-less.

When Klose was not used from the beginning (four times), or substituted from the starting 11 (three times), Germany opted for an enviously talented attack with three from Thomas Müller, Mario Götze, Mesut Özil and Andre Schürrle in the three most attacking positions. To pin any of their front three down into a particular position was difficult. Any time Klose was withdrawn from a game, most of us spent our time trying to work out who would play where. Unlike when France's Giroud was frequently withdrawn, we knew that Benzema would take over as central striker with the substitute, normally Griezmann, taking his position on the left. Applying this easy rationale to the Germans was not so straightforward – even adding the movement arrows to the graphic below was tricky as you were never quite sure of their patterns.

Germany's organisation and synergy allowed these players the fluidity to affect the game as they felt they needed to. Even Müller, their primary goal threat, wasn't a number nine in the traditional sense, and was utilised both centrally and from the right throughout the tournament. Added to a technically sound midfield, and a high defensive line, Germany could spend the majority of games in the opponent's half.

I read (in lots of places) that Germany were "efficient", "organised" and "mechanical", all of which is true, but to limit this to a national stereotype is inaccurate and unfair. It was like they took the best of German organisation, game-sense, and discipline, and mixed it with modern features of football around defending high, taking risks, and attacking fluidly in numbers. They were expertly organised, yet instantaneously adaptable and fluid – a mix that is extremely difficult to master.

Germany's 4-3-3 v. Portugal

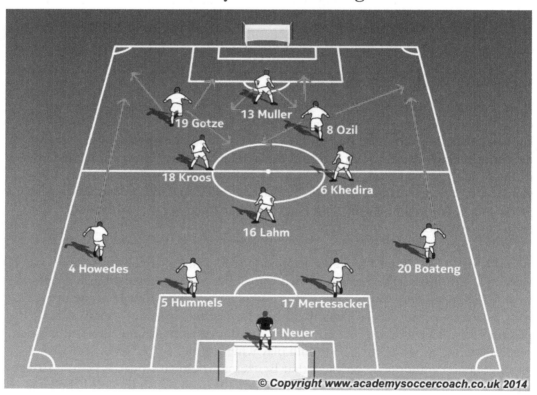

Four-Five-One

With the proliferation of teams playing 4-2-3-1, you could expect a certain number of transitions to both 4-4-2 and 4-5-1, especially when teams were not in possession. I guess the popularity of the system is because of its adaptability and ability to morph into different shapes as suited.

At times, against Russia, South Korea's 4-2-3-1 looked very much like a 4-5-1 out of possession, although that can be said for many of the teams defending compactly with this formation.

Greek Emperors

If some teams' 4-5-1 was a mere consequence of their defensive shape, Greece used it wholeheartedly. Following their success at the 2004 European Champions, 4-5-1 became the staple Greek football diet. They were happy to play without the ball, defend well and resolutely, and hope to utilise counter-attacks or, more likely, set-pieces, to score. This blueprint saw them record five 1-0 victories in qualifying, and keep a total of eight clean sheets, conceding only four goals. They prepared for the World Cup Finals with two further clean sheets in friendlies against Nigeria and Portugal.

From a tactical point of view, you could appreciate why coach Otto Rehhagel felt he needed to keep to a formula that had put the Greeks on the football map. Although competent in possession around their back four, and into their deep-lying midfielder, their technical ability and creative spark higher up the pitch was rarely seen. What they did have was a game plan to allow them to defend resolutely, transition quickly upon losing possession, and delay any threats of being counter-attacked themselves.

Although they were well used to the system and the tactic of containing and playing without the ball, you could say that it took them three games to perfect it – beating the Ivory Coast following a goal from a quick regain of possession and a penalty-kick.

In their 0-0 result against Japan, the plan to play compactly and defensively got them a result, even with only 25.3% of possession. This was vintage Greece; all that was missing was a set-piece goal to steal the game from a Japanese side that could not turn three-quarters of the game's possession into a goal.

We did see, however, how this tactic can have its limits and could somewhat go out the window once they conceded, and in particular when they conceded early in games. Against Colombia, that very thing happened. After some trickery from impressive Colombian winger Cuadrado, rampant left-back Pablo Armero squeezed in a right-footed finish to put Greece behind after just five minutes.

Pre-match, the game was pitched as being the technically dominant Colombians controlling the ball, and the willing spoilers Greece happy to concede possession. Once the opening goal went in however, the tables were turned. Colombia allowed their technically inferior opponents to have possession, where their lack of attacking creativity saw them start to play quite directly (playing into Colombian hands). Earlier we mentioned that England could struggle to break down compact defences, and would tend to go around or over them, and the Greeks fell into this trap. Without the quality to chase the game, and without an efficient Plan B, the Colombians cruised to an eventual 3-0 victory.

Greece 4-5-1 v. Japan

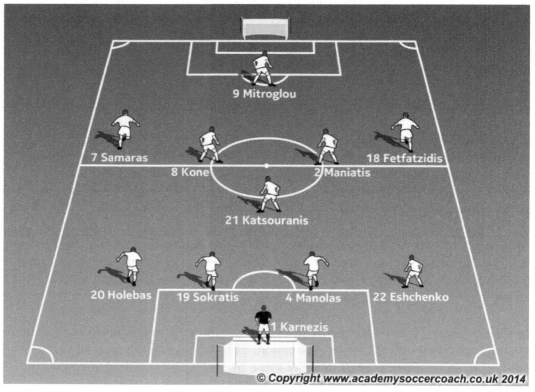

The Greek 4-5-1 formation has been a common theme for the Europeans, hoping to replicate their famous European Championships victory in 2004. This line up held Japan to a 0-0 draw with only a quarter of the possession count – one of the lowest recorded at a World Cup.

Four-Four-Two

Four years ago, I wrote a magazine article about the "death" of 4-4-2, in particular following England's struggles using this formation compared to the other top footballing nations. This was an *absolute statement* that I should never have used. Sure, 4-4-2 has seen a real decline since the 1990s, but it will be back, and no doubt it will come back a bigger, better, more well-oiled machine.

During the 2014 World Cup, 4-4-2 did make a reappearance, though in different guises that we may have been used to during the 1990s.

The Colombian Box

By the time Colombia met Uruguay in the Final 16, James Rodriguez had made a name for himself. He had scored in all three of Colombia's group games, made two official assists (I will add a third following his 'dummying' of the ball for Armero's goal against Greece!) and was virtually involved in all of his side's goals. By the end of the tournament, he was the winner of the *Golden Boot* (top goal scorer). No other player scored or assisted more goals at the 2014 World Cup (eight).

During these group games, Colombia used a 4-2-3-1 formation, with Rodriguez utilised as an out-and-out number 10. Of course he roamed – his ability allowed him to do this, but he did his damage against teams in central attacking areas.

With this in mind you would expect Uruguay to have a plan to negate the impact of the Colombian number 10 in those areas, just like defensive midfielder Egidio Arévalo Ríos had done against Wayne Rooney earlier in the tournament. To negate this, coach José Pékerman changed formation and used Rodriguez from the left-hand side, with the opportunity to drift inside and affect the game in an area he knew best. And affect the game he did. This 2-2 shape in midfield, commonly used by Brazil through the years, is often termed a "box" midfield.

Colombia's 4-4-2 v. Uruguay

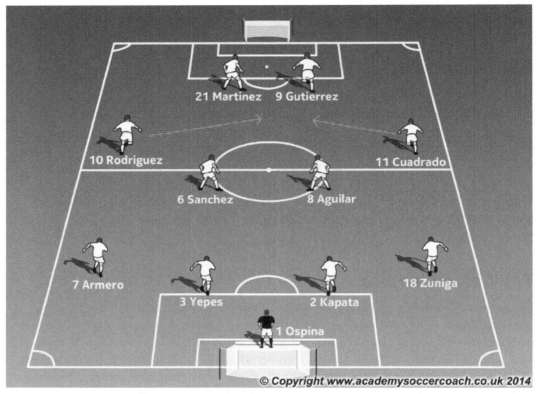

On paper Colombia's 4-4-2 looked quite traditional, but their use of two wide players coming in from wide to take up central positions, particularly Rodriguez, meant it was anything but traditional.

His start position from the left allowed him not only to drift inside, but to do so with some stealth and Maxi Pereira, the Uruguayan right-wing-back, was not going to track him inside. The further presence of two strikers, Jackson Martinez and Teófilo Gutiérrez, allowed them to occupy Uruguay's three centre-backs, who were reluctant to vacate their central defensive positions.

We all marvelled at the goal itself – the touch, turn and volley – which was voted the best goal at the World Cup. What we need to appreciate further, however, is the movement in the preceding seconds that allowed him to avoid detection and being marked, to drift into an area between Uruguay's midfield and defenders. There is a wonderful video of the goal on YouTube, shot from the crowd that shows this stealth and evasiveness from markers.[1]

James Rodriguez's Possession v. Uruguay

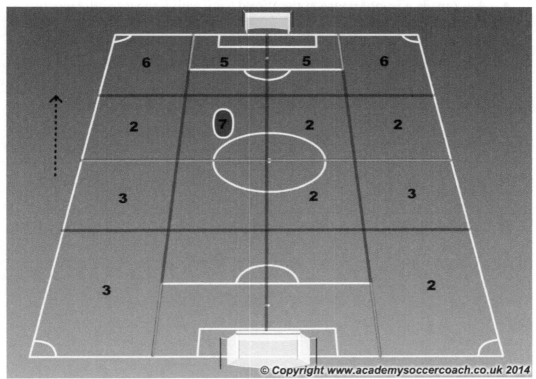

© Copyright www.academysoccercoach.co.uk 2014

Although with a starting position from the left of a midfield four, it is clear from the illustration above that Rodriguez's movement patterns took him into central positions, with seven individual possessions in central left areas, and nine in total centrally.

Summary

- The 2014 World Cup presented us with wide tactical variety.
- We also saw lots of tactical fluidity, where teams either changed formation recurrently, and players shifted positions, and many occurrences of players affecting the game beyond the traditional duties of their chosen position.

---

[1] See video at http://www.youtube.com/watch?v=iGPZf_aF82M

- Although 4-2-3-1 was the most popular formation for the second World Cup running, there is a feeling that it is becoming stale.
- Russia, France, Argentina and Germany all utilised a 4-3-3 system, although all in differing ways.
- The Greeks once again showed their preference towards a defensive 4-5-1.
- 4-4-2 made a reappearance at the World Cup, with Uruguay and Argentina most notably using it.
- Columbia used a 4-2-2-2 variant of 4-4-2 in their knock-out game against the Uruguayans to free up space for star player James Rodriguez.

4

Back Threes and Fives

"A man with new ideas is mad – until he succeeds!" (Marcelo Bielsa)

If the large-scale presence of 4-2-3-1 was no surprise at the 2014 World Cup, the proliferation of teams playing with three centre-backs was. The 2010 event in South Africa offered very little indication that this would be the case. Sure, in Italy's Serie 'A' in recent years there has been significant use of the 3-5-2 formation, particularly with Juventus as they claimed the Scudetto using the system under Antonio Conte.

At the World Cup Chile, Mexico and the Italians themselves all seemed likely to use variants of a back three. Several other nations were to follow this path also; something we will look at over the coming pages.

It was as much of a surprise that Italy chose *not to* use the 3-5-2, considering the success of the formation under coach Cesare Prandelli when reaching the final of Euro 2012 (of the sixteen teams that took part in the European Championships finals that year, Italy were the only ones to play with a back three). With the resurgence of the system in Italy, Prandelli reverted to it for the only time in their must-win contest against Uruguay in their last game in Group D. Although Italy are renowned for being especially flexible tactically, they were unimpressive in their opening games against England and Costa Rica, and their World Cup campaign was to cost Prandelli his job after the competition.

Italy's 3-5-2 v. Uruguay

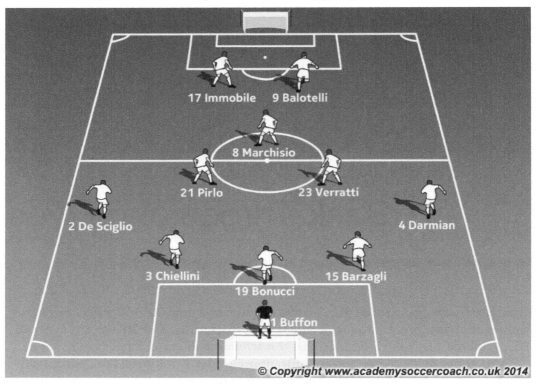

17 Immobile   9 Balotelli

8 Marchisio

21 Pirlo   23 Verratti

2 De Sciglio   4 Darmian

3 Chiellini   15 Barzagli

19 Bonucci

1 Buffon

In their final group game against Uruguay, Italy reverted to the 3-5-2 that served them well at Euro 2012 – a sign of their faith in the system, using it in a must-win game, although one they ultimately lost.

Like we have said countless times throughout this book, tactics evolve and react to trends in the game. I remember being on my UEFA 'A' Licence course and the room scoffed when it came to the unit where we studied the topic of lining up with three-at-the-back and the use of a sweeper. That way of playing was perceived as 'dead'. We should have known that - one day - it would come around again. And in the 2014 World Cup in Brazil it did exactly that.

Since the late 1990s we have seen an astronomical rise in the number of teams that play with a single striker. As midfield domination has become more and more important, coaches have sacrificed strikers, reverting from two to three-man midfields. With only one striker to play against, there is little need to play with three centre-backs as a 3 v 1 in this area meant you would be significantly overloaded in another.

Recently, however, there has been a clear rethink of the value of 3-5-2 formations. The use of wing-backs who work defensively at full-back, and with licence to attack as wingers, saw teams who played the popular 4-2-3-1 or 4-3-3 struggle to set up to cope with them.

The Back Line

It is, often, not particularly easy to pigeon-hole formations that use three centre-backs. We can play the numbers game once again by dwelling on whether we should call systems 3-5-2, 5-3-2 or even, in the case of the Netherlands and Chile, 3-4-3 or 3-4-1-2. In reality the teams we saw at the World Cup will have used back threes, back fives, and situationally (and ironically) even back fours.

Threes, Fours and Fives

Just like teams that play 4-2-3-1, 4-3-3 or any other formation, all teams will set up and interact differently. Chile chose to defend almost purely with a back three (although they played with a back four in a 4-4-2 in their first group game against Australia), whereas Uruguay and Costa Rica were happy deploying a back five. Mexico, on the other hand, saw their back three often morph temporarily into a back four.

Uruguay's 5-3-2 v. Italy

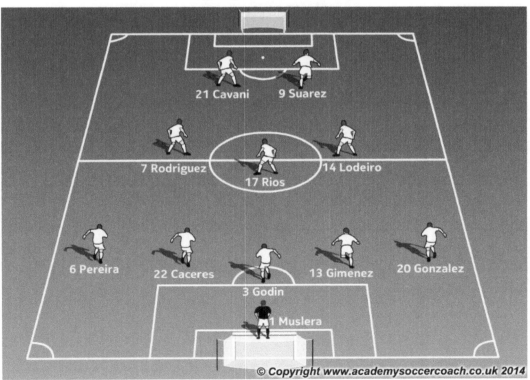

© Copyright www.academysoccercoach.co.uk 2014

Chapter 4

Regardless of team shape and formations, players move and interact based on the position of the ball and the opposition, as well as the immediate danger and the state of the game. It is important to note, as we will see below - with the graphic of the Netherlands against Costa Rica - back lines can shift between three, four and five players. Tactics and formations are situational and will depend on the team's need at a particular time.

Out of Possession

Playing with three central defenders will predictably make a team quite strong in central areas, but sometimes quite vulnerable in the wider, less occupied zones. In their semi-final clash, Argentina routinely tried to get runners down the sides of the Netherlands' back three, through their attacking trio of Higuaín, Messi and Lavezzi. It is normal when out of possession, therefore, for the team's wing-backs to join their three centre-back colleagues and produce a five-man defence. Teams that set up with three central defenders will often transform their back line into playing with a crescent shape containing either four or five individuals.

In the case of the Netherlands, their numerical superiority in central defensive areas allowed them to press players aggressively in and around their penalty area. They could leave their 'zone' (their line of three) to deal with any danger they saw fit. We often saw Stefan de Vrij, Ron Vlaar or Martins Indi leave their positions to put pressure on a striker or advanced midfield player, without the fear of being exposed, like a centre-back would be when playing in a two-man partnership.

Netherlands Changeable Defensive Line

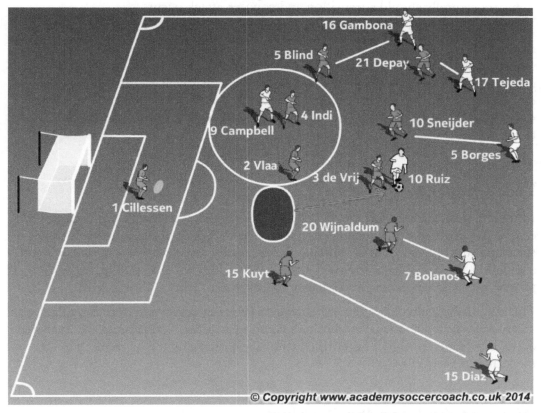

In the above image we see a great snapshot of a three-man centre-back defence defending using differing shapes. The Dutch back three converted into a back five with wing-backs Dirk Kuyt and Daley Blind dropping into full-back positions. This five changed to a four once de Vrij left his right centre-back position to press Brian Ruiz. Within 30 seconds, the Dutch defended with a back three, five and then a four. Above, de Vrij could leave his other centre-back colleagues to defend 2 v 1 against Joel Campbell, who is temporarily offside. All the other players are marking a space but with designated players to press should they receive the ball.

In Possession

In possession, we often saw teams who play with three centre-backs push home their central numerical advantage in possession by driving with the ball out of defence. Mexican sweeper, Rafael Márquez, captaining the side at his fourth World Cup finals, particularly showed this against hosts Brazil and against Cameroon.

Márquez, a good technician as well as defender was comfortable in driving forward in possession, knowing that both his centre-back colleagues, Héctor Moreno and Javier Rodríguez, had secured the space he vacated should a transition occur. The presence of three centre-backs, rather than two, also ensures there are greater numbers centrally should a transition and counter-attack occur.

The presence of three centre-backs subsequently allows a team's wing-backs to attack with much more freedom. Chile provided a great example of this in Brazil, where their wing-backs were free to attack aggressively as they saw fit. During their game against the reigning champions, Spain, right wing-back Mauricio Isla came close to scoring following a shot from left wing-back Eugenio Mena – a situation where both wing-backs found themselves in the Spanish box, even with a two-goal lead!

Wing-Backs

In the 3-5-2 formation, and its variants, the position(s) of a side's wing-backs is crucial. With these teams loading central areas with lots of bodies, the wing-backs, as their title suggests, are almost fulfilling the position of two players – a full-back and a winger. They are obliged to provide the team's width when attacking, but also to provide defensive numbers and balance in defence.

This use of the wide player can either lead to teams being over-run in these flank areas, as we noted above by Argentina's tactic against the Netherlands, or cause the defending team a problem in terms of whose responsibility it is to mark them or track their forward runs.

Wing-Backs Pose the Problem

The use of wing-backs pushing back opposition wingers was never so blatantly evident than in the Group A game between Mexico and Cameroon. The Africans never really got a grip on the game and the Mexican wing-backs pushed the normally attack-minded African wide players, Benjamin Moukandjo and Eric Choupo-Moting, back into full-back positions. Mexico's forward-thinking approach saw them reduce Cameroon to virtually playing a back six when out of possession, meaning that support for their lone striker and talismanic captain Samuel Eto'o was very hard to come by. I noted two instances, one in each half, where Cameroon had won the ball, managed to smuggle it forward to Eto'o, and, like the best player in the school playground, he attempted to receive it and take on the Mexican defence on alone. Of course, with three central defenders and a defensive midfielder in the shape of José Juan Vázquez to contend with, plus the lack of support from the Cameroonian wide attackers, Eto'o found this predictably impossible.

In contrast to this, Bosnia and Brazil were happy for the most part, to let their full-backs deal with the wing-backs of Argentina and Mexico respectively during their group games.

Cameroon Struggling to Deal with Mexican Wing-Backs

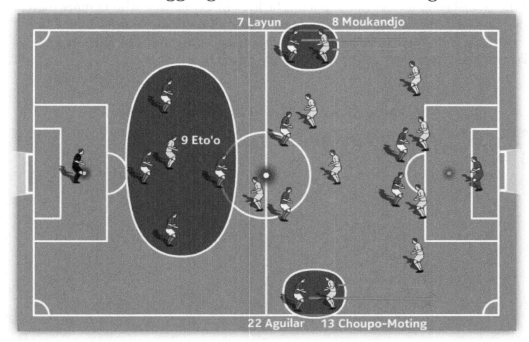

Cameroon wide players Benjamin Moukandjo and Eric Choupo-Moting being forced into deep, defensive positions by Mexican wing-backs, Miguel Layún and Paul Aguilar. Not only did this reduce Cameroon to essentially playing with a back six for large parts of the match, their counter-attack was largely nullified as Eto'o was greatly out-numbered.

Midfield

Different formations and shapes lend themselves further to the different use of midfield players. The beauty of the 3-5-2 is that a team can still dominate the midfield by using three players in central areas. The Italian 3-5-2 that we looked at above had two holding midfielders and one attack-minded 'number 10' in the shape of Claudio Marchisio. Both the Netherlands and Chile used an even more attack-minded number 10 in the shapes of Wesley Sneijder and Arturo Vidal respectively in their 3-4-1-2 formations.

If we invert Italy's midfield three, we end up with the midfield shape that Argentina used in their opening game against Bosnia. They used the traditional operation of one holding midfielder in Javier Mascherano with two further midfield players in Maxi Rodríguez and Ángel Di María who had greater licence to get forward and involve themselves in attacks.

By fielding a midfield three, teams could compete with a four-at-the-back opposition in the crucial central areas of the pitch. The likes of Costa Rica, who at times played a 5-4-1, would have a line of four midfield players, though the widest of the four, Bryan Ruiz and Christian Bolaños would tuck in and play quite centrally. Again allowing their wing-backs to provide genuine width in attack.

Argentina Central Midfield Three v. Bosnia

The shape of Argentina's midfield three was typical of what you would expect from a 3-5-2 formation, with a designated holding midfielder in Mascherano, and two forward thinking players in Di María and Maxi Rodríguez.

Italy Central Midfield Three in 3-5-2 v. Uruguay

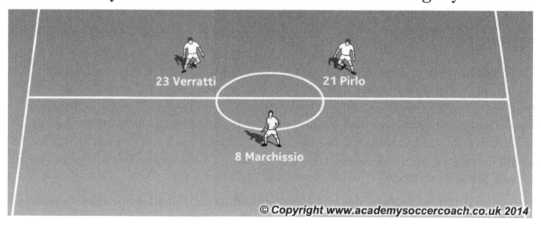

Against Uruguay, Italy inverted the shape used by Argentina, fielding a central midfield pairing of Verratti and Pirlo, allowing Marchisio to play further forward.

Chile Central Midfield Three in 3-4-3 v. Spain

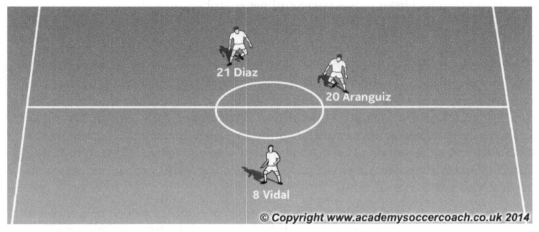

For much of the World Cup, Chile used Díaz as their holding midfield player, Aránguiz was their multi-purpose midfielder, and this allowed Vidal to play as high up the pitch as possible in support of their two strikers.

Costa Rica Central Midfield Four v. Netherlands

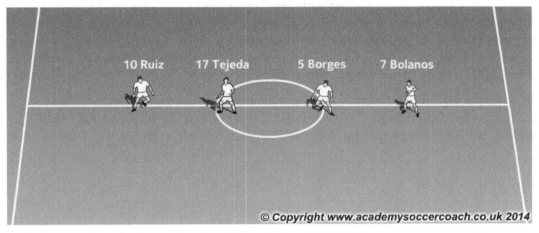

With Costa Rica playing with a back five, their midfield shape was a narrow four, again blocking central areas with numbers.

Forward Players

Arguably one of the most important impacts of the rebirth of the 3-5-2 at the 2014 World Cup was the resurgence of the strike partnership. Tactical analysts had begun to look at the famous combination of number nines and tens as something from the past, possibly never to be seen again with any consistency. The trend in football until this World Cup had been to use fewer and fewer strikers.

The popularity of the 4-2-3-1 has forced forward players to become more than simply goalscorers. In his wonderful tactical book, *Inverting the Pyramid*, Jonathan Wilson traces the fortunes of 1998 World Cup starlet Michael Owen, noting that "the modern forward… is far more than a goalscorer, and it may even be that a modern forward can be successful without scoring goals." Midway through his career, with teams prioritising one multi-functional striker, a 25-year-old Owen, with an international goal-scoring record of almost one goal in every two games, was unable to find a Champions League club to invest in his services. In fact, footballing fashion looked more like it was heading for striker-less 4-6-0 formations rather than playing with a strike partnership.

At times during the 2014 World Cup however, we not only saw two strikers paired together, we even saw the use of three strikers, or certainly three notable attackers. Both Chile and the Netherlands used a designated front three in a 3-4-1-2 formation.

Using Three Strikers

When Costa Rica and the Netherlands lined up against each other in the quarter-finals, there was a sense (again) of David versus Goliath. The Dutch had earned plaudits early in the tournament by convincingly toppling champions Spain, coming from one-down to win 5 – 1; a performance which contained a wonderful display from clinical strike partnership Robben and van Persie.

Both teams lined up with formations containing three central defenders. The Netherlands adapted their 3-4-1-2 to a more obvious 3-4-3, and Costa Rica fielded an unusual 5-4-1 – a formation that was seldom used in Brazil.

Costa Rica 5-4-1 v. the Netherlands 3-4-3

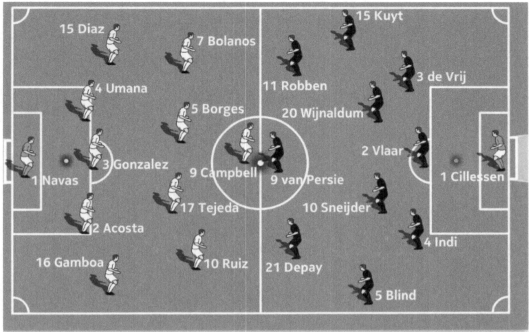

© Copyright www.academysoccercoach.co.uk 2014

The Costa Ricans, in their familiar role of David, had navigated an extremely tough group by beating Uruguay, Italy, and drawing against England to finish top of Group D. Their tactically astute coach, Jorge Luis Pinto, had set them up in a mixture of 4-5-1 or 3-5-2 system or a mixture of both. They reverted to a definite 5-4-1 against the Dutch, who themselves altered their 3-4-1-2 to a 3-4-3. By playing three out-and-out attackers in the form of Arjen Robben and Memphis Depay flanking Robin van Persie, van Gaal was attempting to occupy the three Costa Rican centre-backs, in itself justifying Pinto's use of five defenders.

Netherlands Front Three Occupying Costa Rican Centre-Backs

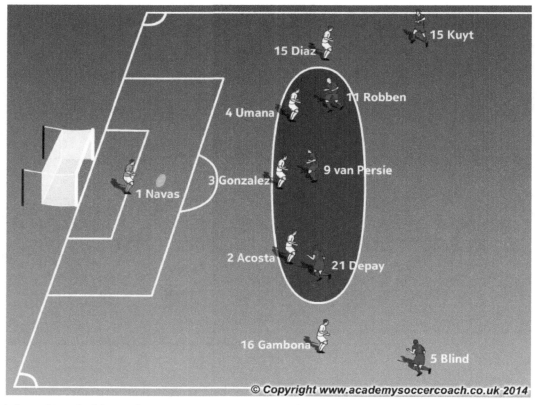

Three Dutch forwards, Robben, van Persie, and Depay, were set up to occupy three Costa Rican centre-backs Umaña, Gonzalez, and Acosta, affecting their ability to be an attacking force from defensive areas.

Predictably the Dutch had the vast majority of the ball – and so they should have. After all a squad littered with title-winning medallists from all over Europe, should have, if nothing else, the technical ability to dominate a game against a group of players who played their club football across the world's lower leagues.

We spoke earlier in this book about game-changers – those moments, decisions or players that affect games and either make tactics work or spoil them completely. This game had those in abundance. Costa Rican goalkeeper Keylor Navas was forced into making countless saves, Sneijder hit a post from a well-taken free-kick and van Persie not only missed the ball completely with the goal at his mercy, he also saw a low, driven shot take a deflection off two defenders and rebound back off the crossbar.

Although the Netherlands had all these chances, Costa Rica's game plan was being implemented quite nicely. The number of bodies they employed in central areas –

three centre-backs and four central midfield players – saw the Dutch often reverting to playing from side to side, and once the ball came into the likes of Robben, a force of will and force of bodies managed to get blocks in and frustrate the Bayern Munich man and his colleagues.

Although defensively solid (when organised), Costa Rica could offer very little in terms of their counter-attack. Similar to Cameroon and Eto'o, Joel Campbell found himself isolated against three centre-backs, with Costa Rica's only genuine chances coming from set-plays. As the game wore on, the world and television cameras increasingly looked towards van Gaal to see if the much-respected tactician would wield his magic again and turn a frustrating draw against World Cup minnows into a win. On social media people hypothesised whether the Dutch would commit a centre-back forward, like Márquez did for Mexico, or maybe revert to a 4-3-3 to get players in between the Costa Rican back five and midfield four, in a similar way to the games they won against both Australia and Mexico (see following illustration) earlier in the tournament.

Netherlands 4-3-3 that Finished v. Mexico

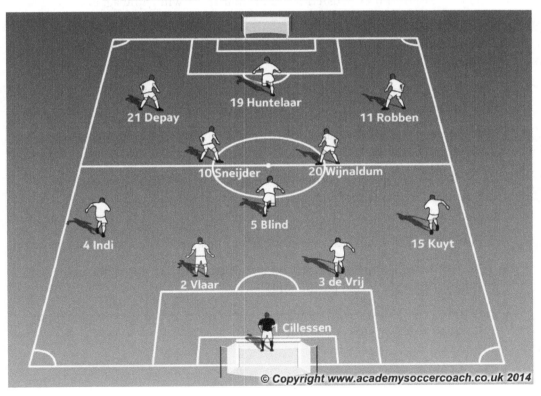

Chapter 4

When trailing to Mexico in the World Cup 2014 Quarter-Final, Louis van Gaal chased the game by changing from 3-4-1-2 to his more traditional 4-3-3, something he chose not to do against Costa Rica.

Tactically, van Gaal did none of those things – his most notable contribution in terms of changing the game saw him substitute goalkeeper Jasper Cillessen for Tim Krul moments before the penalty shoot-out (a change that although labelled a "tactical" masterclass in the media, was in fact more of a psychological one. Krul could be seen telling Costa Rican players that he "knew" where their penalties would go as the substitution looked to get into the heads of Pinto's team). This wonderful tactical battle was settled on penalties, which eventually saw the Dutch through to the World Cup semi-final.

Summary

- Teams playing with three centre-backs increased dramatically at the 2014 World Cup.

- Italy reverted to their trusted 3-5-2 in their must-win game against Uruguay.

- Defensive lines containing three centre-backs often morphed into formations with a back line of three, four, or five, depending on the situation.

- Teams with three centre-backs are stronger centrally, but can be exploited in wide areas.

- Wing-backs have a dual-purpose of providing attacking width and defensive cover and balance.

- Cameroon struggled to cope with the attacking Mexican wing-backs with their wide attackers often dropping into a back-six.

- The 3-5-2 and its variants allowed teams to use numbers in the vital central midfield area, though teams used different shapes of three and four players.

- One of the most important outcomes of the rebirth of the 3-5-2 is the resurgence of the strike partnership.

- At times, three designated attackers were even used, a huge turnaround in the trend towards striker-less formations.

5
Players, Players, Players

"Tactics don't win games, players do!" (Football cliché)

Over recent decades, tactics have changed immeasurably – the abundance of formations we have looked at is testament to that. If team tactics have changed greatly, so too have the roles and responsibilities of players playing within these upgraded and updated systems and strategies.

We must remember that it is not tactics alone that decide games. At any one time it is 11 players on the pitch that are making decisions, performing technically, and approaching the game psychologically. A sending off, a goal scored or conceded, or an injury can force a rethink in any game plan.

Tactics are obsolete without players who are capable of executing them. Greece, for example, do not have the quality of personnel or creativity to play Spain's tiki-taka or Chile's relentless attacking style. Likewise expressive, physically diminutive teams like Mexico or Spain could not play the direct and set-play orientated football that the Greeks do.

Positions

Below, we will look at how the evolution of football tactics has changed the roles and responsibilities of the players who play within them. We will analyse, position by position, the main trends that have altered the way we look at (and stereotype) players positionally.

Chapter 5

Goalkeepers – Footballers Not Just Line-Keepers

We demand a lot from the modern goalkeeper. It is no longer sufficient for a top level keeper to simply stand on his line, make saves and distribute the ball as far down the pitch as possible. Although he still needs to make match-winning saves (we will look at the importance of goalkeepers' shot-stopping at the World Cup later in this chapter), he needs to have the passing, receiving, and distribution skills to rival his outfield team-mates. The modern goalkeeper now uses his feet seven times more than he did in the early 1990s.

In *Making the Ball Roll*, we looked at the turning point for goalkeepers in the modern game, and ironically this came from the rather dour World Cup Italia '90:

> *In 1992, the "back-pass" rule was introduced into the Laws of Association Football. For those young enough not to remember football pre-1992, it was perfectly acceptable for a goalkeeper to pick up a pass from his teammate. This was often used as the ultimate means to time-waste legally and often led to dull games, which came to a head at the World Cup: Italia 1990.*

> *One game springs to mind from that tournament. England were leading Egypt 1-0 in Cagliari, and in the meantime - 400km away in Palermo - the Republic of Ireland and Holland merely needed a draw for both to qualify from Group F. With the scores level at 1-1, the game petered out in the closing stages leading to the Irish goalkeeper, Pat Bonner, constantly rolling the ball out to his defenders, before happily collecting the back pass to kill the game. Against Egypt in the same tournament, Bonner allegedly had the ball in his possession for a total of six minutes!*

Bonner himself confessed that this new law changed the role of the goalkeeper forever – and noted that those who could not cope with the new technical demands of the goalkeeper's game, quickly faded away. Six World Cups later however, we now have goalkeepers that are more than capable of using their feet as well as their hands, *and* arguably as well as their outfield team-mates. A FIFA study that analysed 43 games from various competitions between September 2004 and May 2005 found that not only did goalkeepers have to use their feet more than they did, but that they actually used their feet even more than their hands:

FIFA Study of Goalkeeper Interventions

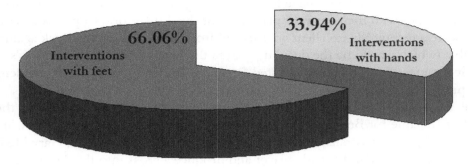

Germany's Manuel Neuer, France's Hugo Lloris, and Chile's Claudio Bravo all showed comfort levels with their feet that saw them consistently exit the safety of their penalty boxes to start or join in the build-up to their team's attacks, or to receive the ball to relieve the pressure on their outfield team-mates. In a frantic game against Brazil in the Round of 16, where both teams relentlessly pressed each other, Chile's Bravo received 16 back-passes to help relieve pressure on the team caused by Brazil's high pressure tactics.

Out of possession, modern goalkeepers are quick to leave their goal line to 'sweep' up behind their defenders. This was most evident against Algeria, as we looked at earlier, when German goalkeeper Neuer had 17 touches of the ball outside his penalty area. For Germany to play their modern brand of attacking football, and to maintain a high defensive line, they needed Neuer to play this type of game. There was even a joke that went around football circles that in Germany's quarter-final versus France, Neuer and Lloris would clash for possession in midfield, given their propensities for leaving their box!

Centre-Backs – More Than Big and More Than Strong

Traditionally, we have looked at centre-backs as defenders only. They tended to be big and strong and were often described affectionately as being "no-nonsense". When dealing with opposition strikers, coaches would instruct these defenders to "let them know you are there", which is basically code for an over-aggressive approach to the duel.

Centre-backs are, however, evolving. Sure, for the most part, they are still big, strong and can be aggressive. They are, after all, the last line of defence in front of the goalkeeper, will often take physical charge at set-plays, and they need to defend against direct play. France's Mamadou Sakho for example, has the physique and traits of a traditional centre-back, yet his biggest criticism is that he is not technical enough and liable to make mistakes when in possession.

Chapter 5

More is now demanded of centre-backs as footballers. Not only are they defenders, they are the starters of attacks, have licence to forage forward, and even influence important games with their forward play. Two of the 2014 World Cup's most iconic images were a technically excellent goal scored from a David Luiz free-kick against Colombia (which was to be the deciding goal in the tie) and Vincent Kompany's defensive interception against the United States, which led to him running the length of the pitch to get on the end of a fast-paced counter-attack – that he himself started! The Belgian's gamble and forward surge in the 89th minute almost won the Round of 16 game for Belgium in normal time (they eventually secured victory in extra-time). Against Australia, while playing at centre-back in a 4-3-1-2, Gary Medel even managed to overlap his wide player and produce a cross into the Australian box.

Rather than simply being responsible for launching the ball from back to front, centre-backs now regularly have possession statistics comparable to midfield players. Australian centre-back Matthew Spiranovic, whose team lost all three of their games at the group stages, had a 100% pass completion rate against World Champions Spain. According to FIFA's end-of-competition pass accuracy statistics, four of the top six players were centre-backs (we must acknowledge, however, that the passes defenders are required to make are considerably less risky than, say, a number 10 trying to play a complicated through ball).

2014 World Cup Highest Pass Accuracy

Rank	Player	Nation	Position	Pass %
1	Garay	Argentina	Centre-Back	94%
2	Mertesacker	Germany	Centre-Back	93%
3	Indi	Netherlands	Centre-Back	91%
4	Luiz Gustavo	Brazil	Deep-Lying Midfielder	91%
5	Vlaar	Netherlands	Centre-Back	91%
6	Lahm	Germany	Midfielder / Full-Back	91%

Such are the technical capabilities of modern centre-backs that, along with being trusted in possession, they are also often utilised at full-back. Such was the confidence of German coach Joachim Löw (whose tactics relied on advancing, attacking full-backs) in the ability of his centre-backs that he regularly utilised Jerome Boateng, Benedikt Höwedes and Shkodran Mustafi as the team's full-backs. It was only injuries that forced Germany to redeploy expert full-back Philipp Lahm back into his natural right-back position, having spent the early games of the competition as their deep-lying midfielder. Belgium, a recent breeding ground for gifted footballers, also happily utilised natural centre-backs at full-back. Jan Vertonghen's excellent contribution in attacking areas against the U.S.A. in their Round of 16 match saw him have four attempts on goal, and eight attempted crosses.

Wing-Backs – Assisting

The trend of forward-thinking full-backs is a growing one. In previous generations, we looked at Brazil, with Roberto Carlos and Cafu both powering into attacking areas, as being the exception. Now, almost every team will use their full-backs as offensive as well as defensive players.

For this section I have purposefully used the term 'wing-back' rather than 'full-back' in the title. This is not just to include those playing as natural wing-backs like Chile's Eugenio Mena and Mauricio Isla in a 3-4-1-2, but to include those who play as forward-thinking full-backs even when part of a back four.

Traditionally those selected to play in full-back positions were small and often technically limited. Their main job was to mark the opposition winger and their attacking threat was generally about feeding the ball to their own winger, or directly into the team's strikers.

The modern full-back however is much, much more than that. They attack as much as they defend, they create as well as intercept, they offer offensive options as well as defensive cover. As mentioned in Chapter 2, For France, Didier Deschamps had the choice between selecting either Arsenal's Bacary Sagna or Newcastle's Mathieu Debuchy. With little to choose between the two, Deschamps selected Debuchy because he saw him as being more dynamic in forward areas, and having a better final pass. Netherlands wing-back Daley Blind was the second highest provider of assists at the 2014 World Cup with three, behind only Chile's wide attacker, Juan Guillermo Cuadrado, and German midfielder Toni Kroos

Full-Back / Wing-Back Assists During World Cup

Overall Rank	Player	Team	Assists
=2	Daley Blind	The Netherlands	3
=3	Daryl Janmaat	The Netherlands	2
=3	Marcelo	Brazil	2
=3	Philipp Lahm	Germany	2
=3	Ricardo Rodriguez	Switzerland	2
=3	Serge Aurier	Ivory Coast	2

With the importance of attacking full-backs to modern tactics, it puzzled me why Russia - in their opening game against South Korea - used an attacking full-back like Yuri Zhirkov in a wide attacking position in a 4-3-3. There is some argument that this tournament left some of the older generation coaches behind, and the feeling in Russia was certainly that Capello's tactics were outdated. Had Zhirkov been German, Croatian or French, he would almost certainly have played as an attacking left-back, giving his side an extra attacking option from deep.

Deep-Lying Midfielders – From Defence to Attack

One of modern tactics greatest trends has been the introduction and specialisation of the deep-lying midfield player. By definition these are players that will command a holding position in the central midfield areas. Arguably France's Claude Makélélé popularised the position, although maybe his particular set of attributes suited the defensive role required in formations such as 4-3-3 and 4-2-3-1 once teams had routinely sacrificed a striker in a 4-4-2 for a more defensive midfield player.

José Mourinho, discussing the role of the Frenchman in his Chelsea team, stated:

"If I have a triangle in midfield – Claude Makélélé behind and two others just in front – I will always have an advantage against a pure 4-4-2 where the central midfielders are side by side. That's because I will always have an extra man. It starts with Makélélé, who is between the lines. If nobody comes to him he can see the whole pitch and has time. If he gets closed down it means one of the two other central midfielders is open. If they are closed down and the other team's wingers come inside to help, it means there is space now for us on the flank, either for our own wingers or for our full-backs. There is nothing a pure 4-4-2 can do to stop things."

Positions Before Introduction of Specialist Deep-Lying Midfielder

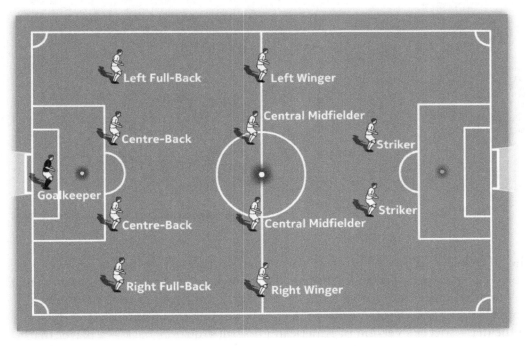

Modern Formation Containing Deep-Lying Midfielder

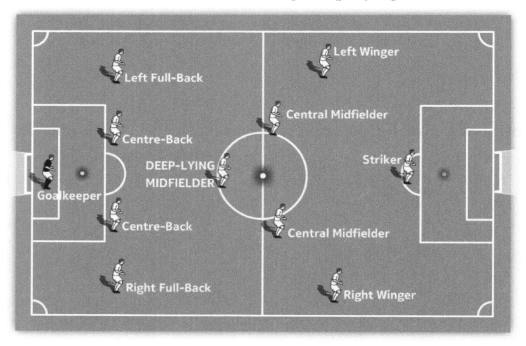

The 'Makélélé Role', as the position affectionately became known, has however evolved as quickly as it was established. There are few "Makélélés" left – players that are purely defensive and with a focus on destruction rather than construction in a football sense. The 'defensive midfielder' is now definitely a technical, deep-lying midfielder – soccer's version of American Football's 'quarter-back' – a player that looks to control games *with* the ball, start attacks, and set the tempo for the game.

During the 2014 World Cup, more and more technical players took up these types of positions, rather than the 'destroyers' that were previously deployed in these midfield roles. Spain's Sergio Busquets and Argentina's Javier Mascherano are often described in disparaging terms for their destructiveness, and although both are renowned for their tackling and defensive positioning, they are both technically excellent. Let us not pretend that the defensive qualities of these players are suddenly unimportant – they are. Mascherano's role in the Argentine midfield was a major factor in the South American team's journey to the final without falling a goal behind in any of their games (crushingly, the last seven-minute period of extra-time in the Final against Germany was the only time Argentina were a goal behind during any point in the competition). Intercepting the ball rather than making crunching tackles are now the order of the day, and their positioning when out-of-possession remains vital for the smooth running of their teams.

When their team was in possession, we saw these deep-lying midfielders often lying even deeper, dropping into central defensive positions to allow centre-backs to step forward with the ball, and kill teams who tried to press them. Díaz did this frequently for Chile, as did Germany's Philipp Lahm, amongst other deep midfielders throughout the competition.

Deep-Lying Midfielder Dropping Between Centre-Backs in Possession

When centre-backs are in possession, the deep-lying midfielder frequently drops in between the two centre-backs, allowing the player in possession to advance forward, offering a support option behind the ball, and offering defensive security should they lose possession.

As well as players like Díaz and Lahm in this position, we also found that midfield players noted for their attacking ability, and therefore their excellent technical skills, were used more and more in this position. Yohan Cabaye, Steven Gerrard, and Axel Witsel who are just as, or even more, accomplished as attacking midfielders were used as deep-lying players for France, England and Belgium respectively.

We can also add another breed of deep-lying midfielders in the shape of individuals who made their names as *diminutive* number 10's – Luka Modrić and Ivan Rakitić played together as the deep-lying double-pivot for Croatia, and we also looked at South Korea's Ki Sung-Yueng's capabilities in that position earlier in this book. All made their name in football as clever, attack-minded players who played in pockets of space behind the forward players. In 2001 Roberto Mancini, a former *trequartista* (number 10) himself, wrote his thesis for his coaching badge with the Italian FA. He noted that the number 10 had "a scarce presence in the defensive phase"[1] – how much this has changed in 13 years.

Multi-Purpose Midfielders

The evolution of more traditional number 10's into more deep-lying positions can be seen as a direct result of the change in the style and requirements of the *trequartista*.

Traditionally a team's number 10 would look to exploit the space on the edge of the opposition's penalty area – known as 'zone 14'. With the large-scale presence of one, if not two, deep-lying midfielders reducing the space in central areas, these players have had to evolve, adapt, and go elsewhere to cause opposition defences damage. The 10 is no longer simply "a player who positions himself in the central zone between the midfielders' line and the attackers' line", as noted by Mancini, he must now have the traits of a winger (we are increasingly seeing number 10s being called "inside wingers") – he must be able to dribble, run with the ball, play centrally or out wide in either left or right areas – and crucially, he will be asked to contribute to the defensive phase of the game.

---

[1] Translation thanks to soccertranslator.com

Zone 14

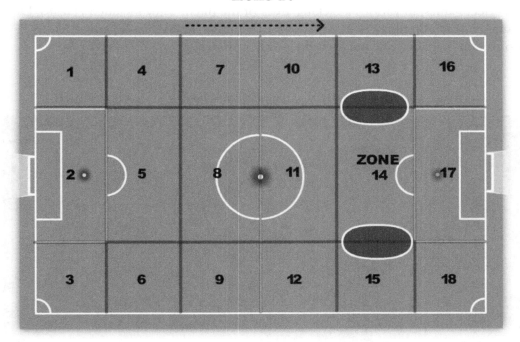

© Copyright www.academysoccercoach.co.uk 2014

Zone 14 is the attacking central area of the pitch located on the edge of the box, and traditionally the source of lots of goal-scoring chances. With Zone 14 being increasingly protected by midfield players, those who traditionally exploited Zone 14 now tend to drift all over attacking areas. Terms like 'Zone 13.5' are increasingly becoming used to describe the shaded areas above to indicate the growing influence of attacking players trying to exploit areas to the sides of Zone 14 and the deep-lying opposition midfielders.

There has been a real blurring of the lines between those who play as number 10s and those who play as wide attackers. Natural number 10s have the traits of wingers and wingers have the traditional traits of number 10s – they seek spaces in crowded central areas to exploit, rather than exclusively looking for 1v1 situations, and have more in their technical armoury than simply dribbling and crossing. The blurring of these lines allows teams that play 4-2-3-1 to rotate the specific positions of the attacking midfield three. Brazil, for example, tended to play an attacking midfield three of Neymar, Hulk, and Oscar, although all three consistently appeared in different positions during different games, and often during the same game. The truth is that coaches are now more comfortable in allowing the flair and creativity of their players to be used, along with their evolving honesty and work-rate, much more than used to be the case.

The very best of these attacking players at the World Cup had the ability to appear, and affect games, in various attacking areas of the pitch. They included Hazard, Di María, Neymar, Sterling, Messi and a raft of German attackers who consistently showed this capability throughout their time in Brazil.

Ángel Di María Individual Possessions v. Switzerland

In their quarter-final against Switzerland, Di María was selected to play from the right, although we see from his individual possession chart (via Prozone) that he consistently popped up all over the pitch, particularly in the Swiss half.

Not only are attacking midfield players becoming more rounded position-wise, we are also seeing a minor yet significant increase in natural wingers playing as central midfield players. Again Di María and his midfield colleague Maxi Rodríguez are good examples of this, as is the all-round German star Bastian Schweinsteiger. With the growing propensity for 'inside wingers', we may well see more natural wide players evolving into central midfielders. Stereotypical central midfielders would play off two-touches, switching the play and doing most of their 'box-to-box' running without the ball. In contrast now, however, there is a growing trend for midfield players who pick the ball up in central areas and drive forward in possession. Natural wide players, like Di María, with these skills already honed, may begin to influence central positions more and more.

Non-Goalscoring Strikers

When we analyse strikers, the first attribute next to their name is their goal-scoring statistics. Historically, we were told that every team needed a number 9 who scored goals and was judged on little else. It did not truly matter whether they worked hard out-of-possession - putting the ball in the back of the net was their job. Because of the fame and glory of the position, and the exquisite knack needed to score goals by the hatful, kids grew up dreaming of being their team's star striker. The mantle, however, has shifted.

At the 2014 World Cup, not only was the tournament's top scorer an attacking midfield player, only three out-and-out strikers, Enner Valencia (Ecuador), Karim Benzema (France) and Robin van Persie (The Netherlands) made the Top 10. Brazil, a nation famed for its number nines, had Fred spear-heading the attack; he managed only one goal in six appearances. Critics were quick to pounce on Fred, and although he provided only a limited contribution to the host-nation during the tournament, he played in a Brazilian team that was set up to allow team-mate Neymar to be the star man. Miroslav Klose (Germany) scored two as did Colombia's Jackson Martínez. Gonzalo Higuain scored once for Argentina, as did Wayne Rooney for England and other top strikers like Romelu Lukaku (Belgium), Fernando Torres (Spain) and Eden Džeko (Bosnia).

Top 10 Goal Scorers at the 2014 World Cup

Rank	Player	Country	Position	Goals
1	Rodríguez	Colombia	Attacking Midfield	6
2	Müller	Germany	Attacking Midfield	5
3	Messi	Argentina	Attacking Midfield	4
=3	Neymar	Brazil	Attacking Midfield	4
=3	van Persie	The Netherlands	Centre-Forward	4
4	Schürrle	Germany	Attacking Midfield	3
=4	Robben	The Netherlands	Attacking Midfield	3
=4	Valencia	Ecuador	Centre-Forward	3
=4	Benzema	France	Centre-Forward	3
=4	Shaqiri	Switzerland	Attacking Midfield	3

As I completed the above table, I must admit I struggled writing the term "attacking midfield" to describe all those wonderful players. It is like I was unduly pigeon-holing wonderfully flexible, versatile, universal midfield players into one category. The description is merely for convenience, rather than a widespread categorisation of players that, frankly, cannot be put into one neat descriptive box. After all, how do you categorise Xherdan Shaqiri, Arjen Robben and Thomas Müller into one opportune position?

The False 9

We briefly mentioned Spain's previous use of the False 9 earlier in this book. Cesc Fàbregas, we noted, was utilised in that position for their 2012 European Championships victory.

We could argue that Fàbregas was Spain's version of Barcelona's False 9, who of course used Messi so successfully in this position under the reign of Pep Guardiola. In 2014, we saw the German adaptation of the False 9, especially in their utilisation of their top scorer, Thomas Müller, who simply cannot be categorised as a striker, winger or attacking midfielder – he is a combination of them all. Former German international Mehmet Scholl described him best as not a False 9, but a "Wild 13" (Müller's squad number) given his propensity for popping up almost anywhere.

Just like our conundrum of pigeon-holing attacking midfielders above, it is difficult to bracket the False 9 also. In the simplest terms, he is somewhat of a hybrid between a striker, an attacking midfield player and a winger. His start position may be as a traditional number 9, but he drops off into attacking midfield areas and into wide positions. This leaves a real problem for opposing central defenders and it becomes a significant challenge for defenders to work out who is responsible for picking him up – and when.

Arguably the U.S.A. used, or at least attempted to use, Clint Dempsey (the multi-purpose midfield player) as a False 9, though Germany provided, by far and away, the best example from the World Cup in Brazil. Although they did use World Cup goalscoring record-setter Miroslav Klose as an out-and-out number 9, they quickly reverted to a False 9 system when he was not selected, or had been substituted.

Indeed it was quite humorous to listen to old-fashioned television commentators scramble to get a grasp of the German shape, once Klose was substituted. Again the pigeon-holing began, when really it was not necessary. Such was the German faith in the striker-less False 9 system that 36-year-old Klose was the only true striker they included in their entire World Cup selection squad. If any goal was to justify this approach it was their most famous of all – Mario Götze's extra-time World Cup Final winner.

Germany's False 9 System and the World Cup Winning Goal

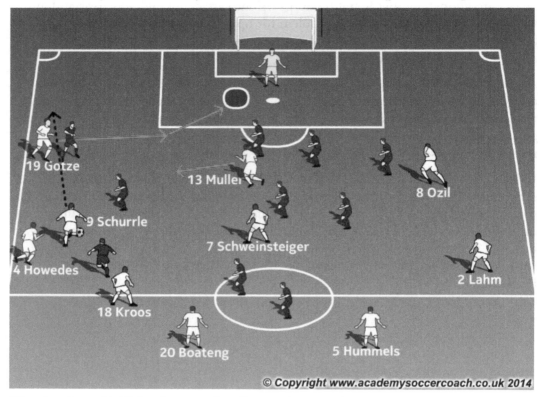

The above image highlights the point when Germany's André Schürrle picks up possession from a Tony Kroos pass, before driving forward down the left-hand side of the pitch. As he drives, Müller moves out of his central area, rather than attack the penalty box like a traditional number 9 would. Mario Götze, stationed wide on the left when Schürrle gained possession, makes a run inside and eventually scores the World Cup winning goal from the shaded area in front of goal.

'Special' Players

Throughout this book we have noted that it is not just tactics that win games, but players, decisions, twists of faith, etc. In Brazil we also saw that some very high profile games and tactical battles were won by single moments of brilliance from individual players.

Winning Games

This player may be the 'X-Factor' player – that one who can produce something special to win a game, almost on his own. He can likely do the things that his team-mates cannot, and also produce moments that the opposition simply could not set a game plan for. It is a mixture of individual brilliance and, to a certain extent, the tactics that allow these players to flourish. These tactics may involve building the player into a team structure, or building the team structure around the player.

Lionel Messi helped Argentina through a very sticky group, with winning goals against very stubborn opponents in Bosnia and Iran – and also a brace against Nigeria. Similarly James Rodríguez secured Colombia's passage from the group stage into the knock-out stages of the World Cup, and was heavily involved in virtually all of their goals, and often in spectacular fashion. In a very even match, it was Uruguay's Luis Suárez who scored two exceptionally well-taken goals to defeat England 2 - 1. Brazil never quite looked the same once they lost their talismanic special player Neymar through injury. The quality of these players, and their ability to change games through technique and sublime finishing, means their position in their respective teams allow them to win games that are otherwise hard-fought and tight.

Messi's Last Minute Winning Goal v. Iran

The image above is a freeze-frame at the point Lionel Messi makes contact with the ball for his winning goal in the final seconds of their hard-fought group game against Iran. At the point of

contact, all eleven Iranian players were in or around the box, yet remained powerless to stop the goal, including two players in very close proximity to the special Argentine.

In an effort to stop special players, teams frequently resorted to negative tactics of either man-marking or double-marking these players, or occasionally bending the laws of the game by consistently fouling them. In the game between Brazil and Mexico, which included an astonishing 54 fouls (a tournament record), both star players, Neymar and Rodríguez, were subjected to frequent, 'rotational fouls' (four on the Colombian, six on the Brazilian). By rotating the players doing the fouling, the players from both teams completely avoided being yellow-carded for their fouls on both number 10s.

Saving Games

We could argue a case for the effectiveness of any player in any position – we did so above with Javier Mascherano and we could rightly note that it was Germany's collective brilliance all over the pitch that won them the entire competition (with their full-back-cum-deep-lying midfield player, Philipp Lahm, amongst their best).

While we can note the effectiveness and worthiness of full-backs and midfielders, there is something more spectacular about players who score goals from very little, and also those who prevent goals when seemingly they should have no chance.

The 2014 World Cup was notable for some exceptional goalkeeping performances. We spoke about Neuer, Lloris and Bravo (above) in a 'footballing' context, but we must also note the importance of keepers making excellent saves and preventing goals.

As good as Costa Rica were tactically in Brazil, their goalkeeper Keylor Navas kept them in games with inspiring performances and saves. Arguably the most stand-out individual goalkeeping performance came from the U.S.A.'s Tim Howard in their Round of 16 game against Belgium. The American made a World Cup record-breaking 16 saves during the tie, and was therefore the most highly ranked goalkeeper in terms of shots saved. When we look away from the statistics, another goalkeeper, although not on the list below - Mexico's Guillermo Ochoa - made a string of exceptional saves in their Group A encounter against Brazil.

Top Ranking Goalkeepers – Number of Saves World Cup 2014

Ranking	Goalkeeper	Country	Saves	Conceded
1	Howard	U.S.A.	27	6
2	Neuer	Germany	24	4
3	Enyeama	Nigeria	22	5
4	Navas	Costa Rica	21	2
5	M'Bolhi	Algeria	20	7
5	Benaglio	Switzerland	20	7
5	Romero	Argentina	20	4
8	Cillessen	The Netherlands	17	4
8	Dominguez	Ecuador	17	3
10 =	Bravo / Ospina	Chile / Colombia	16	4

Summary

- Tactical changes in recent times around formations and strategies have led to a change in the roles and responsibilities of players in different positions.

- Goalkeepers like Neuer, Lloris and Bravo are as comfortable with the ball at their feet as they are with the ball in their hands.

- Centre-backs that were traditionally big and strong are now technically proficient and join in attacks.

- Full-backs behave as wing-backs and are required to be dynamic and forward-thinking, as well as offering defensive balance.

- Deep-lying midfield players, whether playing as a single or double-pivot, contain players who are creative and not simply destructive.

- Midfield players have become more multi-purpose. They rotate positions; central players have the skills of wingers; wingers play in central areas; and we see number 10s playing wider and deeper than they traditionally have done.

- Strikers are required to contribute more than goals and cannot be 'just' goalscorers. Only three of the 2014's World Cup's Top Scorers were out-and-out strikers.

- Germany put their faith in a False 9 system which culminated in Mario Götze's World Cup winning goal.

- Games are frequently not won by tactics but by special attacking or defensive players.

6
Possession-Based Football

"You want possession, you want to attack. Some teams can't or don't pass the ball. What are you playing for? What's the point? That's not football. Combine, pass, play. That's football" (Xavi Hernández)

Since roughly the turn of the century, possession-based football was seen as the driving force behind all successful football – a clear absolute statement that is difficult to justify. Amidst football's admiration for keeping the ball, passing and probing - a search for solutions was taking place behind the scenes. The football fraternity was not just going to sit back and watch teams 'out-possession' them to defeat. Like Sacchi's suggestion earlier in the book – with every revolution, there is a counter-revolution. While Spain had passed the world into submission in recent years, other coaches and teams were looking at a way of adapting or defeating the seemingly undefeatable model.

With or Without the Ball?

The theory that possession of the ball wins you games, and is the only way of winning games, is now in serious doubt. After the 2014 World Cup, it is clear that there are many ways of progressing through tournaments, whether this is through dominating the possession statistics, as Germany did (we will look at Germany's capabilities in possession more below), playing without the ball and counter-attacking, as the Netherlands did so well, or mixing and matching a possession-based and a defensive game, something that took Argentina to the final. (Incidentally, Argentina topped the possession statistics from the Group Stages, although against Iran - with the Middle Eastern side defending for their lives and having the competition's lowest possession percentage rates - Messi and co. had almost 80% possession, an outlier that shot their average skywards).

Of the four teams that took their place in the World Cup semi-final slots, all four stretched widely across the possession statistics table. While Germany's percentage of possession during the competition was second only to, you guessed it, Spain, The Netherlands came in at 20th, sandwiched between African duo, Nigeria and Ghana. Argentina and Brazil were ninth and eleventh respectively when it came to their possession percentages. Quarter-finalists Colombia (23rd) and Costa Rica (29th), plus Greece (25th) and Algeria (31st) who exited at the Round of 16 stage, failed to reach the top 20.

Percentage Possession & Round of Elimination – Top 20

Rank	Nation	% Poss	Round Elim.	Rank	Nation	% Poss	Round Elim.
1	Spain	61.4	Group	11	Brazil	53.3	Sem Fin
2	Germany	59.9	Winners	12	South Korea	52.5	Group
3	Japan*	59	Group	13	Belgium	52.3	Qtr Fin
4	Italy	57.6	Group	14	Russia	51.8	Group
5	France	56.5	Qtr Fin	15	Portugal	51.1	Group
6	Ivory Coast	55.8	Group	16	Croatia	50.6	Group
7	Bosnia	55.4	Group	17	Mexico	49.3	R.16
8	Chile	55.3	R.16	18	Switzerland	48.9	R.16
9	Argentina	55	Final	19	Nigeria	48.9	R.16
10	England	54.3	Group	20	Netherlands	48.5	Sem Fin

Japan's game against Greece pushed them higher in the possession standings as they had almost 75% of the ball against a Greek team content to squeeze a positive result playing without the ball.

By analysing the possession statistics from the World Cup, we do see a shift in emphasis from how much possession a team keeps, to what they do when they are in possession – a form of quality over quantity. Of the top ten teams in terms of pass percentage, six of them exited at the group stage, three of which – Spain, Japan and Italy – make up the top four.

Spain and Italy are amongst the teams highest in the table for percentage possession and pass success rate (85.5% and 89.1% respectively) yet they watched the Round of

16 games from home, while Algeria, having completed only 68% of their passes and having attempted 800 fewer passes than Spain and 600 fewer than the *Azzurri*, not only went further in the competition, but went as close to anyone in overcoming the Germans by utilising a game plan that involved *not having the ball*. Perhaps the most telling stat of all was how The Netherlands stormed through their "group of death" despite having a total of only 39.5% of the possession – only bettered (if that is the correct word) by Iran's measly 30.4%.

Furthermore, Diego Torres, a Spanish journalist who has written about José Mourinho's approach to big games when he was coach of Real Madrid, quoted the Portuguese as saying, "Whoever has the ball is more likely to make a mistake. Whoever renounces possession reduces the possibility of making a mistake." The idea then of renouncing possession in an effort to win games is a growing one. Is the importance of possession therefore 'dead'?

Tiki-Taka

The notion of 'tiki-taka' is a recent popularisation, but is not something that is 'new'. It has been brought back into world focus by the success of Barcelona and Spain over the last decade or so. By definition the tactic involves a team dominating possession by using lots of short passing sequences and combinations. It demands a high level of technical expertise, not just to pass and receive, but to seek spaces, take risks in possession, and stick religiously to a philosophy that was 'their way'. By dominating the ball, not only could the opposition not score, but it demanded that they stayed physically and mentally alert. If they could not do this, the technical dominance of the team playing tiki-taka would open them up and they could almost score at will.

With the tiki-taka style, every footballer or wannabe footballer under five foot ten now had an argument as to why they could have a major place in the game, amongst clubs who insisted that size was the determining factor in becoming a successful player. We now routinely watch diminutive players like Xavi Hernández, Andreas Iniesta, David Silva and Juan Mata dominate games through technique and nous rather than brawn and brute force.

Tiki-Taka 2014

The central aspects of tiki-taka are not new. Although it has been made popular in Spain through the rise of Pep Guardiola at Barcelona and the all-conquering national team under Luis Aragonés and Vicente del Bosque, the method has been around for much longer than this. The famous Dutch era in the 1970s, led by figures such as Rinus Michels and Johan Cruyff, popularised a type of *Total Football*, exporting it to Spain through the Dutch links to Barcelona.

Chapter 6

One of the World Cup 2014's pre-cursors was the question around whether tiki-taka had run its course. This followed comprehensive defeats of Barcelona and Bayern Munich in recent European Champions League tournaments. This judgment of the future of tiki-taka, it seemed, was made after just 45 minutes of football where the Spanish were dismantled in their opening Group B game – ironically against its creators, The Netherlands, whose possession statistics were virtually incomparable to the Spanish; effectively they won the game comprehensively *without* the ball.

Spain v. The Netherlands Possession Statistics

	Spain	Netherlands
Goals	1	5
Attempts	10	14
% Possession	64.5%	35.5%
Successful Passes	540 / 619	276 / 339
Pass %	87%	81%
Attacking Third Passes	86 / 124	54 / 79

We need little more than a quick glance at the statistics from this game, one of the most iconic games of the 2014 World Cup. Spain comfortably dominated all of the possession stats – they had vastly more of the ball, played almost double the number of passes, had a higher pass success rate, and had more passes in attacking, scoring areas. Yet the Netherlands not only won the game convincingly, but had more attempts from less of the ball – prioritising the *quality* of what they did with the ball over the *quantity* of time they had it. Often we see teams with less possession win games – Switzerland beat Spain 1 – 0 in the 2010 World Cup with only 33% of the ball – but rarely do we see a team beaten so heavily having dominated possession so much.

Upon Spain's exit from the World Cup, after two games, there came an extensive hysteria about how tiki-taka was "dead". I even saw one picture that had circulated social media that showed a gravestone adorned with "tiki-taka".

Guardiola's spell as head coach of Barcelona saw the peak of the football world's admiration for the tiki-taka style of football. The gravestone pictured however seemed to poke fun at the perceived downfall of a style of play that had brought such success to Spain, rather than mourn it. Although Guardiola himself scoffs at the "tiki-taka" label, the thinkers, writers and bloggers of the game heralded it as almost the only way the game could and should be played from hereon in. Barcelona and the Spanish national team, we were told, played the game "the right way".

Now, though, the same fraternity are telling us that this is dead. Maybe, however, as tactics inherently evolve, we need to have a clearer look at the bigger picture. It seems only the Spanish ideals of possession football are being criticised and eulogised. If the winners write football history, and this generation of Spanish players have undoubtedly been mass-winners, then their fall is documented almost as dramatically. What we must acknowledge, therefore, which we have done elsewhere in this book, is that it was sequences of short passes that created the penalty to allow Spain to take the lead against the Netherlands, and that short passes created a glorious opportunity for David Silva (which he missed) to put the Spanish 2 – 0 up. If they had gone 2 – 0 up we may well have witnessed another strong tournament from the Iberians. Tiki-taka is not dead – we may simply see it go into hibernation as other forms of game play begin to take the headlines.

The German Revolution

During the 2010 World Cup in South Africa, a new breed of German football was introduced to the world. Young, versatile and clever players like Thomas Müller, Mesut Özil and Sami Khedira had taken the tournament by storm with their team's attacking fervour and incisive networks of passing and quick play - surprising even the German public whose expectations going to South Africa were low.

A rebirth of German football has been a long time coming, forced into existence by tough Deutscher Fussball-Bund (German FA) regulations about the production of youth players and how club academies were to be operated. By the time these young players were professionals in the game they were a part of the principles and system below.

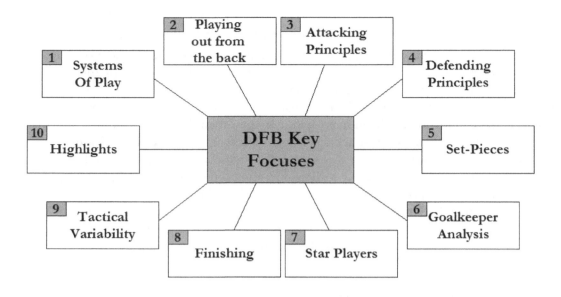

Plan A, B, C, and D

Certain comparisons can be made between the possession-style of the Germans during the World Cup, and that of the Spanish national team in their pomp. Both had goalkeepers that were keen to play out from the back and the intelligent Philip Lahm compared favourably to Sergio Busquets. They both had an abundance of multi-purpose, diminutive attacking midfield players, and their intent to dominate the ball and press opponents high up the pitch was key.

The Germans, however, took their version of tiki-taka to new heights, extended its reach, and added power to its punch. While we have argued that the Spanish team's only recent evolution was the inclusion of an expert central striker in Diego Costa, the Germans were keen to be add many more strings to their bow, and put the "tactical variability" they wrote about into practice on the field of play.

As a default they indeed played out from the back, with goalkeeper Neuer happy to play short to defenders to start attacks from the back. When required, though, they were also happy to play direct football into front players like Müller and Miroslav Klose. They pressed and kept a very high defensive line against Algeria in the Round of 16, but were happy to let the French have the ball in their quarter-final – it is unlikely Spain would ever have seen a game out at 1 – 0 up like the Germans did against France. As Bayern Munich expert, Louis Lancaster would say, they took Spain's Plan A, and added a plan B, C, and D.

Germany Possession Statistics Per Game

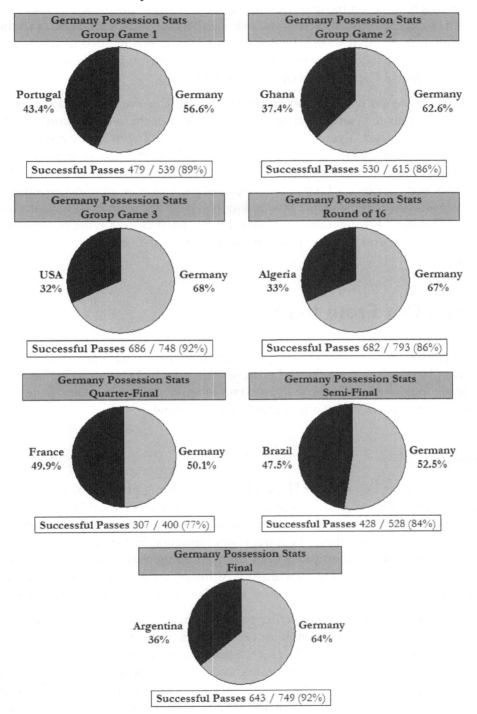

**Germany Possession Stats
Group Game 1**

Portugal
43.4%

Germany
56.6%

Successful Passes 479 / 539 (89%)

**Germany Possession Stats
Group Game 2**

Ghana
37.4%

Germany
62.6%

Successful Passes 530 / 615 (86%)

**Germany Possession Stats
Group Game 3**

USA
32%

Germany
68%

Successful Passes 686 / 748 (92%)

**Germany Possession Stats
Round of 16**

Algeria
33%

Germany
67%

Successful Passes 682 / 793 (86%)

**Germany Possession Stats
Quarter-Final**

France
49.9%

Germany
50.1%

Successful Passes 307 / 400 (77%)

**Germany Possession Stats
Semi-Final**

Brazil
47.5%

Germany
52.5%

Successful Passes 428 / 528 (84%)

**Germany Possession Stats
Final**

Argentina
36%

Germany
64%

Successful Passes 643 / 749 (92%)

As much as they dominated possession in Brazil, their version of possession football was very much based on passing the ball, rather than dribbling. Much of their success has since been attributed to their data collection software that allowed them to get their average possession time down from 3.4 seconds in 2010 to 1.1 seconds per player - thus reducing their use of dribblers (Germany were ranked 27th of the 32 teams at the World Cup in terms of successful dribbles).

The German side did not insist on keeping possession, as the Spanish do. They thoroughly dominated games against teams who allowed them possession – against Ghana, the U.S.A. and Algeria – and they also did so in the final against the Argentinians. Even during these games, where they had 60% plus of possession, they did not dominate on the scoreline – in fact three of those games were level after 90 minutes and a single goal separated them and the U.S.A. in the final group game. Their biggest wins however were resounding – a 4 – 0 win against 10-man Portugal and their famous 7 – 1 demolition of hosts Brazil. Their closest game possession-wise was a close scoring, but comfortable, win over another possession-based team, France.

Playing Out From the Back

Possession-based teams are characterised by a tactic of playing short to middle distance passes, and starting attacks by playing from their goalkeeper, through their defensive players, then midfielders, before working the ball into attacking areas to score goals. Below we will look at the manner in which this is done, and how this philosophy can evolve and change completely mid-game.

France

The French, through goalkeeper Hugo Lloris had a strong philosophy of playing out from the back and through the thirds of the pitch at the 2014 World Cup. Their opponents, as much as any other team in Brazil, varied in terms of quality and reputation. France resoundingly beat minnows Honduras in Group E and exited the competition to eventual champions Germany. Along the way they played competent teams in Ecuador, Nigeria and Switzerland. Although their philosophy remained similar, they often changed tack and how they played out from goalkeeper Lloris.

Once Lloris was in possession, whether through a back-pass, goal-kick, or kick-out, the team would form a shape aiming to use as much of the pitch as possible. The full-backs, normally Evra and Debuchy, would place themselves in wide positions and move towards the halfway line. France's central defenders, normally Varane and Sakho would go towards the corners of the penalty area to receive. Once they did receive, the deep-lying midfielder Cabaye would drop into the space between them to offer support. Their main striker, either Benzema or Giroud (the player who played in this position had a big bearing on the decisions Lloris made) would play as far forward as possible. Valbuena would keep some width on the right, while whoever played from the left would tuck into spaces infield. The two advancing midfielders, normally Pogba and Matuidi would also push forward to allow more space for the defenders and Cabaye to receive.

France Playing Out From Lloris (Honduras)

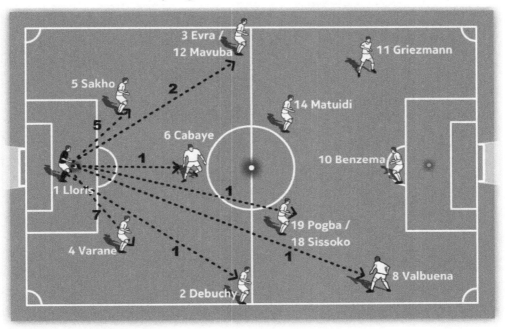

© Copyright www.academysoccercoach.co.uk 2014

Against Honduras, in a game that saw the South Americans reduced to 10 men in the first half, France's game plan of playing out from Lloris through the two French centre-backs was noticeable, and was something that remained a constant throughout their campaign. Rarely did Lloris choose to play out through his full-backs or through his deep-lying midfielder, Yohan Cabaye. Once the centre-backs were in possession, they would feed mainly Cabaye who would play forward or offer diagonal passes to build their attacks.

France Playing Out From Lloris (Germany)

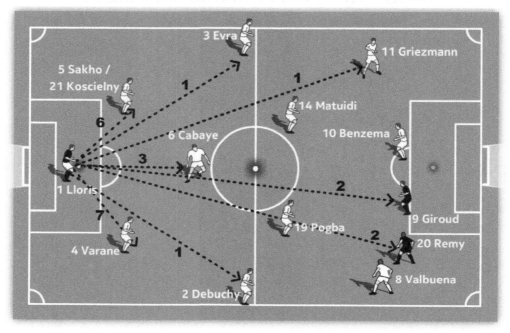

Against Germany, we again see the frequency of Lloris' distribution to the central defenders, but at 1 – 0 down and chasing the game, Deschamps changed the team shape and added attackers Loïc Rémy and Olivier Giroud to the mix (both in black in the diagram as the substitutes were not straight swaps position-wise). Once both these men entered the game after 73 and 85 minutes respectively, and with the French still trailing by a goal, Lloris began playing more directly than usual - into these replacement front players.

France Playing Out From Lloris (Switzerland)

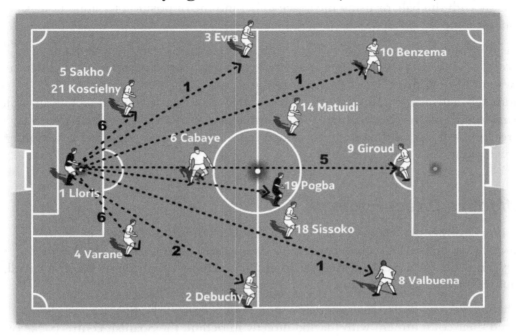

Giroud's presence on the pitch tended to change the approach from Lloris, or at least he varied his distribution a lot more. While playing into Varane and Sakho (who was replaced by Koscielny) was a consistent theme, the French number one also played more directly into Giroud, much more than he would do when Benzema played as a central striker.

Direct Football

Today's culture of analysing football has marginalized direct football as a legitimate match tactic. We deem those who look to go from back to front quickly in uncomplimentary terms, because of a perceived lack of technique, flair and imagination. To praise it is almost slanderous. In the popular mindset, direct football is seen as a defender or a goalkeeper lofting the ball forward either in behind defenders or towards a tall, big, strong striker. We saw, above, from the frequency of passes from Lloris into Giroud that even possession-based teams will – depending on the situation - play directly. This may be because they are losing and chasing a game, or because it plays to the strengths of a team-mate like Giroud. Or, of course, direct play can be used to vary a short-passing approach. The Spanish, for example, have been accused of being slow in evolving their possession-based style and that it has arguably become quite predictable.

Direct football, however, may be this *and more*. It may be a midfield player running directly with the ball, or using the space in behind the opposition to launch quick counter-attacks.

It is not the intent here to defend or overly-criticise teams that use a direct style of football. At the top level of the game, like at a World Cup, a coach's job is to devise a way of playing that utilises a team's strengths, masks their weaknesses, and ultimately wins games. What disappoints football enthusiasts is when technically able teams opt to play unimaginative, direct football, rather than a style where they play through the thirds of the pitch and offer a more creative approach when attempting to win games.

Effective Direct Football

Although direct play has a tarnished reputation, it can be an effective tactic. As much as we praise the Germans for their possession statistics at the 2014 World Cup, arguably their greatest strength was their ability to mix this with direct football, counter-attacking football, and effectiveness at set-plays.

When we analysed the Dutch performance, above, against the Spanish, we also noted their contentment with playing directly in behind the Spanish centre-backs or by playing longer passes on top of Piqué and Ramos as a clear tactic to put the duo under pressure.

Direct from Belgium

The 2014 World Cup was the stage where Belgium was supposed to announce itself to the world as a major power, and a worthy contender for future international tournaments. Much of the build-up to the competition saw their development programmes highlighted for producing a raft of technically excellent players, based around their favoured 4-3-3 / 4-2-3-1 formation.

With all the attacking options available to them, using a 4-2-3-1 was not a surprise, and even less of a surprise considering how they modelled their whole development programme around the system.

One could not help but be a little disappointed in the Belgians and how they utilised their array of available attacking talent. Goalkeeper Courtois was happy to play direct, and if they got into trouble, such as in their opening game against Algeria, they resorted to using the height and heading power of Manchester United's Marouane Fellaini (brought on from the substitute's bench). After their early scare against Algeria, when they had to come from 1-0 down to win 2-1 late in the game, Fellaini became a constant starter in the tournament, and as we see from the graphic below, central to their attacking strategy. It was only in extra-time of their Last 16 encounter against the USA that they really began to take risks, although the open nature of the game assisted them in doing so, and the game would have undoubtedly been finished long before the extra period, but for a string of fine saves from American goalkeeper Tim Howard.

Courtois Direct into Fellaini v. Russia

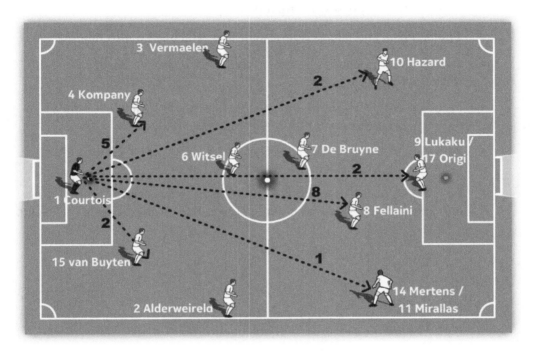

© Copyright www.academysoccercoach.co.uk 2014

From Belgium's second game against Russia onwards, they began to utilise the height of Marouane Fellaini much more. With goalkeeper Courtois in possession, they pushed the number 8 into a much higher position, playing high and direct into him to win headers. The forward players around him would look to pick up the second balls. Although unimpressive aesthetically, this tactic helped Belgium to go further in the tournament than maybe their performances warranted.

Summary

- With the success of the ultra possession-based Spanish national team, other coaches began looking at ways of adapting and defeating the model.

- There is notable evidence from the 2014 World Cup that more games are being won, and more teams are being successful, without the need to thoroughly dominate possession.

- Only four of the top 10 possession teams made it beyond the group stage.

- The Netherlands and Algeria made it impressively through their group stages with less possession than their opposition.

- The Spanish Tiki-taka is not dead, it may well just go into hibernation.

- Germany took Spain's possession model and improved it – adding further strings to its bow.

- France used playing out from their goalkeeper as a tactic, but did play direct at times, especially when Giroud was on the pitch.

- Although direct football is popularly criticised, it can be a very effective tactic.

- Belgium's game plan at the 2014 World Cup was based around playing direct from back to front and utilising the big, strong Marouane Fellaini.

7

Attack, Attack, Attack!

"The trend is to play positively and do everything to win a game rather than merely 'not lose'. Pushing up the field to score was considered more important than playing for safety. Their [the teams] attempts and desire to score were more important than focusing on defensive safety." (2014 FIFA World Cup Technical Report)

From the outset of this book we have looked at the formations and shapes of many of the teams that took part in the 2014 World Cup in Brazil. These formations and approaches, of course, shaped the attacking and defensive strategies (and transition phases – we will look at these momentarily) of the teams that employed them.

When I roughly outlined the chapters of this book before writing it, and prior to the World Cup itself, I placed the defending chapter before the attacking one. Not that I felt that defending would have greater importance, it just seemed like the right place to start. A handful of games into the competition, however, things changed! The FIFA document quoted above showed that attacking football and "risk taking" were a major trend seen in the tournament, much to the organisation's relief after the 2010 competition was remembered for being quite a dull, reserved affair.

The 2014 World Cup saw attacking play catapulted to the fore, in particular during the early group stage matches. These sets of games, compared to their 2010 counterparts, were largely based on teams playing with an attacking intent. The play in South Africa, in 2010, was pretty negative overall by comparison. Throughout this chapter, we will have a look at the goals, how they were scored, and how teams 'transitioned' into attack.

Introducing Transitions

Traditionally, and in some quarters this still exists, we have looked at football as having two phases. The first being when the team is in possession, and secondly when the team is out of possession. Football was simply defined as attacking and defending, when you either had the ball, or you did not.

When we look deeper, however, we find that in-between these moments of possession, there exists third and fourth phases of the game. They are at the immediate points when possession changes hands – or the 'transition' phase.

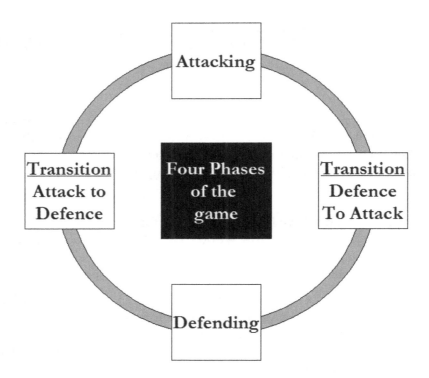

The team that has just lost the ball is in *defensive transition*, where their shape, tactics and outlook must change immediately from attacking to defending. The team that has *just* won the ball is in *attacking transition*, where their focus changes from defending to attacking in one moment.

Transitions are now seen as so important that certain football coaching schools will openly state that the whole game is based around how a team deals with the moments when possession shifts from one team to another. In the following chapter we will look at defensive transition, and in this current chapter, along with analysing the attacking trends in Brazil, we will look at how teams approached attacking transition.

Goals, Goals, Goals

Data from the 2014 World Cup shows a substantial number of positive statistics in relation to goals scored. There are some straightforward statistics that we will draw on here – like how many goals were scored, those scored by substitutes, and what time of the game the ball was put into the net.

Other stats, though, are a little more unclear - to the point where various sources differ in the information they produce. For example, whoscored.com quotes there having been 35 goals from set-pieces, whereas FIFA's official stats claimed 38. Differences in data from several sources also include different interpretations of goals from 'open play' and what constitutes a 'counter-attack'. For consistency then, we will analyse the goal-scoring statistics that are presented in FIFA's Official *Technical Report and Statistics* and also the research from *Sports Path's World Cup Technical Report 2014* (unless otherwise stated), although both reports contain their own variance. Both reports incidentally are available online.

Number of Goals

Overall the tournament saw the joint-highest number of goals ever scored in a single World Cup Finals with 171. This equalled the number scored four tournaments ago when France were victorious on home soil in 1998. That tournament produced an average of 2.67 goals per game (previous World Cups that contained fewer teams have averaged more goals per game, but this is the highest in the 32-team format). 171 goals equates to a scoring rate of just over 13% of shots on goal, which was also the highest percentage at a World Cup.

More goals (32) were scored by substitutes in Brazil than at any other World Cup, the most famous of which was Mario Götze's celebrated winner in the Final at the Maracanã. Incidentally, Götze was also the first substitute to score a World Cup winning goal. The previous record of goals scored by replacements was 23 in Germany in 2006.

There may be several reasons for the proliferation of substitutes' goals in Brazil, none of which can be substantiated tangibly or with a neat statistic to prove it. Modern footballers are now more comfortable with big squads at club level, meaning the role of substitute is more readily accepted and they enter games focused and able to make a significant contribution[1]. Another possible reason is that coaches made good decisions and could identify the individual who could impact upon games best (again this is rather difficult to quantify).

Comparing Brazil 2014 and South Africa 2010 Attacking Statistics

	Brazil 2014	South Africa 2010
Number of goals scored (total)	171	145
Number of goals scored (group games)	136	101
Number of goals scored (knockout)	35	44
Average goals per game	2.67	2.27
Number of matches that ended scoreless	5	7
Number of matches with a single goal	10	17
Goals scored by substitutes	32	15

The data above shows quite clearly how there was a greater focus on attacking play in Brazil, which will surprise nobody who watched both tournaments. What is useful to note, however, is how the early 2014 games started with attacking intent, but became cagier as the tournament progressed. It is likely that the pressure of knock-out football – where one mistake can eliminate you – was greater than for group games, where you typically have other games to rectify any mistakes.

Timings of Goals

In traditional punditry, not a lot of focus is given to the time that goals were scored, unless they are scored exceptionally early or exceptionally late in games. This, maybe, is as much to do with the drama of the goals or the significance of what may be a last-gasp winning goal or equaliser. The USA's time at the competition was at risk of being undone when Portugal equalised in the last minute of the game to earn a 2-2 draw, a late goal that threatened to ruin the US's progression in the tournament. In the Switzerland-Ecuador match, an injury-time winner from Haris Seferović saw the Swiss come from one down to beat the Ecuadorians. Greece forced extra-time

---

[1] While we wondered how Dutch goalkeeper Jasper Cillessen would react following his substitution immediately prior to their penalty shoot-out with Costa Rica, he was actually the first player to jump from the sidelines to celebrate their shoot-out victory.

against the ten men of Costa Rica with an injury-time Sokratis Papastathopoulos equaliser, having piled pressure on the tiring Costa Ricans. Götze's winning goal against Argentina was scored in extra-time with only seven minutes remaining. As mentioned previously, heartbreakingly for the Argentine side - it was the first time during the whole competition that they fell behind in a match.

World Cup 2014 Time Breakdown of Goals Scored

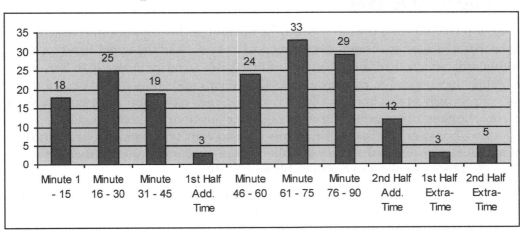

As the chart above shows, a huge percentage of goals were scored in the last fifteen minutes (plus additional time) of games (36 goals, 21% of the total number). Extending that time to reflect the last 30 minutes of games *and* extra-time, we find that 82 (48% of total) goals were scored in that period.

There are several reasons why goals are so frequent in latter periods. From a tactical point of view, teams may take more risks in an effort to win the game, or indeed will commit more resources to attacking in an attempt to equalise. Physically and mentally, teams may also begin to tire and consequentially lose concentration in these periods. Having defended so resolutely against Argentina, Iran were eventually beaten by a 94th minute Lionel Messi winner (as examined in a previous chapter). Conversely, both the USA and Algeria scored late extra-time consolation goals when 2 – 0 down to Belgium and Germany respectively. We can deduce that both European teams became complacent, allowing their opponents to score when the match result was virtually decided.

It is therefore important that, even late in games, even top teams must be physically fit to ensure they can defend, attack, and transition successfully. A high level of physical fitness also helps teams remain mentally fit and retain high levels of concentration and focus.

Goals Win Games

Those driven by statistics in football will point to certain trends (note the use of the term 'trends' and not 'rules') that decide the winners of games. As extraordinary as the 2014 World Cup was in terms of attacking play, the goals reflected many of the trends that we would expect. Let's look at some of these here.

Scoring First to Win

At the top level of the game, the scoring of the first goal is significant. In Brazil, teams that managed to score the opening goal not only had the upper hand on the scoreboard, but also had the advantage of being able to adapt tactically to 'see out' the game; they needed to take fewer risks than their opposition(s) who chased the game. Previously in this book, we looked at the Greek tactic of playing compactly in defence, hoping to win games through a counter-attack or set-piece. Against Colombia, however, the South Americans took an early lead, forcing Greece into having more possession than they actually wanted. And it did not suit their style. The Colombians went on to comfortably win 3 – 0.

The opening games in Brazil initially threatened to obliterate this trend. Of the first 11 games, five of them were won by the team that fell behind (Brazil v. Croatia; The Netherlands v. Spain; Costa Rica v. Uruguay; Ivory Coast v. Japan; and Switzerland v. Ecuador).

This early tendency, however, began to be reversed as the tournament progressed. Only two further teams fell behind and managed to win from the remaining 37 group games (Belgium v. Algeria and Ecuador v. Honduras). In the knockout stages, only one game, The Netherlands' 2 – 1 victory over Mexico was won by the team conceding the opening goal. The eight occasions when teams scored first *then lost* in Brazil, was double that of the 2010 South African tournament.

Touches and Penalty Area

We all admire the long-range goals and mazy dribbles that result in the ball hitting the back of the net. While these types of goals are the most memorable ones, the real truth of goalscoring is significantly more straightforward. Most goals are not from dribblers ghosting past defender after defender to find the net, nor are they from flamboyantly driven strikes from outside the penalty area.

At the 2014 World Cup 58.9% of goals came from a one-touch finish. This stat, of course, includes penalty-kicks (12), direct free-kicks (3) and headers (32). Added to this, 20.9% of goals were from a two-touch finish. In all then, almost four of every five goals were scored from a maximum of two-touches.

While traditional coaching sessions will show players practicing shooting from distance, practising one and two-touch finishing is actually far more valuable. To add further value to the expertise of goal-scoring, the vast majority will also come from inside the penalty area.

Only 19 of the goals at the 2014 World Cup (11%) came from outside the penalty area, although they can often be the most unforgettable. In this book we have already noted Messi's last-minute winner against Iran, Rodríguez's volley against Uruguay and David Luiz's free-kick in Brazil's contest with Colombia. Significantly though, almost 90% of goals were scored from *inside* the box. Add this to the 'touch' statistics, above, and we find that the overwhelming majority of goals come from one or two-touch finishes inside the penalty area, rather than the beloved mazy dribbles and thunderbolt strikes from distance.

Where The 2014 World Cup Goals Came From

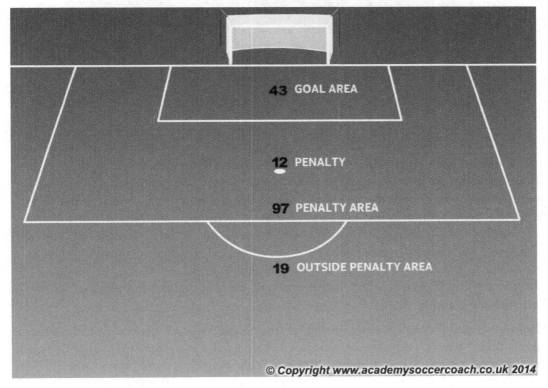

43 GOAL AREA

12 PENALTY

97 PENALTY AREA

19 OUTSIDE PENALTY AREA

© Copyright www.academysoccercoach.co.uk 2014

Assists

During their analysis of the 2014 World Cup, *Sports Path* identified 130 open-play goals scored in what they term the 'gold' zone. This zone includes most of the penalty area, from the outer edges of the six-yard box to the edge of the penalty area, as shown below.

Sports Path's 'Gold' Zone

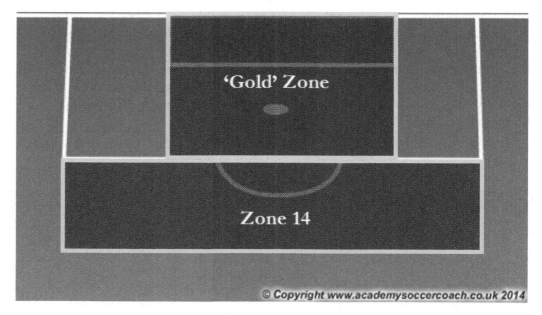

33 of these 130 open-play goals came directly from a final pass from 'Zone 14'. Statistics from domestic competitions in England show that as many as 70+% of goals can be traced back to possession within the central zone outside the penalty area (this may be directly from a pass, or indirectly from possession in that zone during the build-up phase). Although many teams now set up with either one or two defensive midfielders to protect Zone 14, it remained significant in producing over one-fifth of the 2014 World Cup's open-play assists. Add to this the three goals scored directly from free-kicks in this area and we find that the influence of Zone 14 remains alive and well.

Below, we will account for the goals that were scored from set-pieces. Of the other goals, FIFA identified the major sources as being from wing play (37 – slightly more came from the left than the right – 20 and 17 respectively), combination play (26) and defence-splitting passes (17) – the latter two being significant in their involvement in Zone 14.

The sample size for goal-scoring data at any World Cup is quite small. While 64 games may seem a lot, that is less than a monthly number of games during a major domestic league campaign. Of the total 171 goals in Brazil, the assists chart is spread across a colossal 91 different players, the majority of whom contributed just a single goal assist. While 18 players in total claimed two assists in Brazil, only four players managed three or more, as listed below.

Assists Table at 2014 World Cup

Rank	Player	Team	Assists
=1	Cuadrado	Colombia	4
=1	Kroos	Germany	4
=2	Blind	The Netherlands	3
=2	Muller	Germany	3

Set-Pieces (Including Penalties)

When examining the origins of goals, set-pieces[2] always play a significant part in the overall percentage. In fact, either directly or indirectly, set-pieces can account for up to 50% of goals. Set-pieces are points in play where the game has stopped either because of a foul, or the ball leaving the field of play (and restarting with a goal-kick, throw-in, free-kick, penalty or corner-kick). Kick-offs begin both the first and second halves of normal and extra-time, and after a goal has been scored.

The importance of set-pieces at the 2014 World Cup was no different. There were 38 scored in all, 22% of the total number. Not only was the overall percentage of goals scored from set-pieces important, but the significance of these goals were also crucial. Mats Hummels' header from a wide free-kick against France was enough to see Germany into the semi-finals. Brazil, traditionally known for their elaborate open-play goals, scored three of their four knock-out goals from set-pieces.

---

[2] Also known as 'restarts' or 'set-plays'

World Cup 2014 Goals Scored From Set-Pieces

Total	38
After a corner-kick (left) [right]	18 (11) [7]
Direct from free-kick	3
After a free-kick	5
From penalty (excl. penalty shoot-outs)	12
Penalties missed	1

Both these teams – Germany and Brazil – showed clear evidence of the pre-planned nature of their set-piece routines (all teams will have, without question, prepared how they will set up their set-pieces both offensively and defensively). Who could forget Thomas Müller falling over during an elaborate German free-kick routine against Algeria. Even now there are still arguments over whether his trip was a part of the plan or a comical misdemeanour. Two of Brazil's set-piece goals came from a Neymar corner, finding the head of one defender whose aim was to flick the ball on to the back-post area for his central defender partner to score. Against Chile, Thiago Silva flicked on for David Luiz to prod into the net, while against Colombia, this combination was reversed. Italy's Marchisio scored the opening goal from range against England after Pirlo had 'dummied' a pre-planned corner-kick.

Corner-Kicks

The most eye-opening statistic around World Cup set-piece goals was the number scored from corner-kicks (18). 11% of the total 171 goals came from this type of restart compared with 'normal' UEFA statistics of around 2 to 3%. In *The Numbers Game – Why Everything You Know About Football is Wrong*, a book dedicated to applying statistics to football and trying to offer football-related conclusions, Chris Anderson and David Sally produce some really startling facts about the success of corner-kicks in terms of scoring goals. They suggest that a goal comes from a corner only once every ten games. Applying this trend to the 2014 World Cup, you would expect six or seven goals in total (in South Africa 2010, ten goals came from corner-kicks) rather than the 18 witnessed in Brazil. In a single game against Croatia, Mexico scored from two corner-kicks in the space of 11 minutes to book the South American's place in the knock-out rounds of the competition (they also had an earlier one cleared off the line).

The reason behind this high rate of goals from corner-kicks is not something that can be explained with any ease. Teams will have practiced their set-piece routines, while, as we will see in the next chapter, very few teams defended corners with their players marking the posts zonally.

Free-Kicks

Goals scored directly from free-kicks at the 2014 World Cup were minimal – only three found their way from the taker's boot directly into the net. This is compared to a total of five that were scored in South Africa, where the official *Jabulani* match-ball caused goalkeepers many problems with its unpredictable flight. Direct free-kicks resulting in goals can be some of the most memorable moments at tournaments, although their frequency is possibly not as common as everyone expects. Ironically the first 40 games were played at the competition before both Lionel Messi and Xherdan Shaqiri fired in goals from free-kicks for Argentina against Nigeria, and Switzerland against Honduras, respectively – on the same day! David Luiz's spectacular free-kick, taken with his instep, against Colombia, was the only direct free-kick scored during the knock-out phases of the 2014 World Cup.

There were a further five goals scored *indirectly* from free-kicks, like the winning German goal in their quarter-final against France. Typically, throughout the tournament, Germany had more possession than their opponents, but against the French the possession statistics were largely even. Here lies the significance of planning and utilising set-pieces as part of your attacking armoury. In a close game, it may well be how you attack and defend set-pieces that makes the difference.

Penalties

Football is full of variables, unlike many other sports. This unpredictability is a major reason why we love the game. Regardless of tactics, systems, and playing styles, we never truly know what will happen once the ball starts rolling. Set-piece situations reduce the number of variables applicable at that point in the game. Coaches and players can plan and rehearse these restarts more than they can do for any other elements of game.

Furthermore, penalty-kicks reduce these variables even further. A 'spot-kick' boils down to the actions of the penalty taker and the opposition goalkeeper. The taker has significant advantages over the stopper, in terms of the size of the goal (192 square feet) and the short reaction times needed by keepers because of the 11 metre distance between the penalty-spot and goal; the goalkeeper will make a save less than 25% of the time (Brunel University research, published in the Mail Online).

There were 13 penalties given in open-play during the 2014 World Cup, of which 12 were converted successfully, adding weight to the long-standing perception that penalties are easier to score than they are to miss or be saved. The only player to miss an open-play penalty at the 2014 World Cup was France's Karim Benzema in their comfortable 5 – 2 victory over Switzerland.

Penalty Shoot-Outs

Using the penalty shoot-out as a means of deciding a tied game was first introduced to World Cup competitions in 1978, although no game went the duration and into penalties until the 1982 tournament. Since 1982, there have been 240 penalty-kicks taken in shoot-out situations, with 170 of them finding the net (almost 71%).

Only World Cup Italia 1990 (28) had more goals scored from penalty shoot-outs than Brazil (26), with 10 of the penalties missed in both tournaments.

Penalties Scored in 2014 World Cup Shoot-Outs

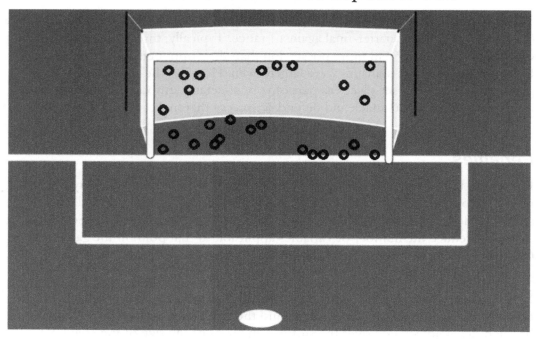

Penalties Missed in 2014 World Cup Shoot-Outs

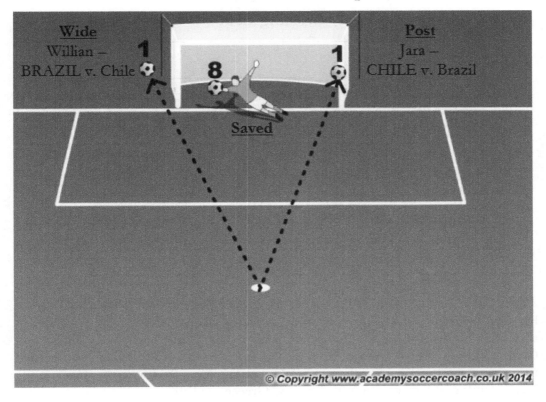

We constantly hear that penalty shoot-outs boil down to mere chance, luck, and how they are football's version of roulette. *It is, however, much more than that.* It involves technical and tactical skills from both striker and stopper, physical issues after potentially 120 minutes of play, and critically, psychological strength. Players have to deal with a significant amount of pressure, especially during decisive kicks where their team may be eliminated should the player miss. From the World Cup shoot-outs, both prior to 2014 and during the 2014 version, there is a huge difference between the conversion rates of players who needed to score to win and those who needed to score to avoid elimination[3].

---

[3] Stats from BBC Sport article *The World Cup Final Penalties Dossier.*

World Cup Shoot-Out Decisive Kicks 1982 – 2010
Scoring to Win / Missing Leads to Elimination

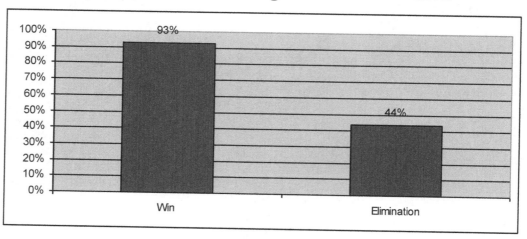

At the 2014 World Cup, only Dirk Kuyt scored when a miss would have signalled his team's elimination. On the two other occasions when a miss would eliminate their team, both Costa Rica's Michael Umaña (v. The Netherlands) and Chile's Gonzalo Jara (v. Brazil) missed. Both players from the 2014 World Cup who needed to score to win the game for their team, Argentina's Maxi Rodríguez (v. The Netherlands and Umaña again (this time v. Greece), did so.

2014 World Cup Decisive Kicks

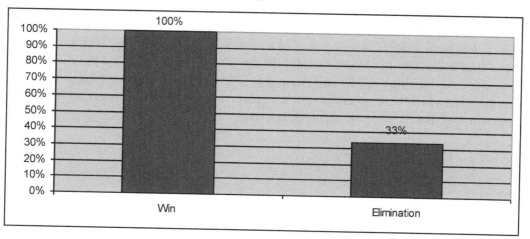

Normally, the most memorable moments from penalty shoot-outs are the highs and lows – the winning penalties and saviour goalkeepers – and then the felons that miss. Players return from their 39-metre walk from the centre-circle to penalty-spot and back as either heroes or villains.

Arguably however, the greatest penalty shoot-out story to come out of the 2014 World Cup took place 44 seconds before the end of extra-time, as Dutch substitute goalkeeper, Tim Krul, replaced regular number one Jasper Cillessen. This ploy worked, disrupting the Costa Rican preparation for, and performance in, the shoot-out. Rumours circulated that the Costa Ricans had prepared a dossier specifically on Cillessen's habits during penalty-kicks – and thus had it ruined by the substitution.

Counter-Attacking

In the last chapter, we looked at significant evidence of teams being willing to play the game *without* the ball. Their method was to defend resolutely and attack quickly once they regained possession. The growing focus on this *attacking transition* saw the FIFA Technical Report comment about its increasing focal point for teams: "Counter-attacking tools were once a tool in a team's armoury, but now some teams base their entire play around such tactics."

Of the 136 goals scored during the group stages, 25 were scored via a counter-attack, and 34 were scored overall in Brazil. Various methods of counter-attacking were noticeable during the tournament, which we can broadly categorise in three groups:

1. A fast player running with the ball into the opponent's defensive area (e.g. Arjen Robben v. Spain).

2. Two or three quick passes forward (e.g. Mertens v. Algeria).

3. A single pass in behind the opponent's defence (e.g. Suarez v England), although this is less common.

A key modern feature of attacking transition is teams identifying strategic areas of the pitch where they will aim to win the ball back to launch their counter-attacks. We normally expect counter-attacking teams to defend deep, inviting the opposition to give them the ball back, as characterised by Greece and Iran throughout their games in Brazil. A really profitable tactic at the 2014 World Cup, however, sought to regain possession much higher up the pitch, hence launching counter-attacks from nearer the opposition's goal.

Counter-Pressing

Every counter-attack begins when the opposition has the ball. When a team places a focus on attacking transition then there must be an acceptance and a comfort when the opposition are in possession. How teams choose to counter-attack, and what areas of the pitch they intend to regain the ball in, differs from team to team.

When aiming to counter-attack, teams would traditionally defend in their own half or defensive third and look for regains to attack from deep. In recent years, though, there has been a growing aim to press higher up the pitch and regain the ball as close to the opponent's goal as possible – the statistics show that the closer to the goal a team wins back possession, the more fruitful it is in terms of goals scored. 70% of Germany's World Cup winning goals came from regaining possession in the attacking third of the pitch. Pressing high up the pitch to regain possession is known as counter-pressing or *gegenpressing* due to its German roots.

Areas of Pitch Where Ball is Regained Leading to a Goal at the 2014 World Cup

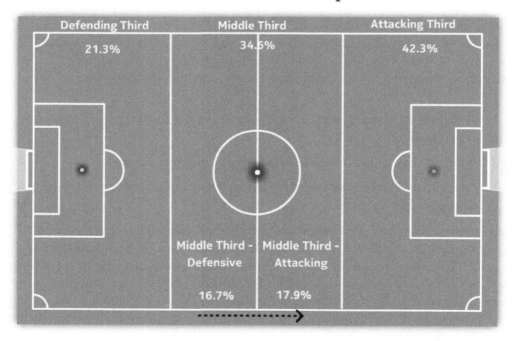

Counter-Attacking from Deep

In *The Numbers Game*, Anderson and Sally present a view of corners being "next to worthless" (they summarised that the average corner is worth only 0.022 goals) "given the risk of being caught on the counter-attack". True to their misgivings, one of my favourite goals from Brazil 2014, and certainly my favourite counter-attacking goal, was a goal from France's Mathieu Valbuena – that had its origins from a *Switzerland* corner-kick.

Valbuena Counter-Attack Goal From Set-Piece v. Switzerland

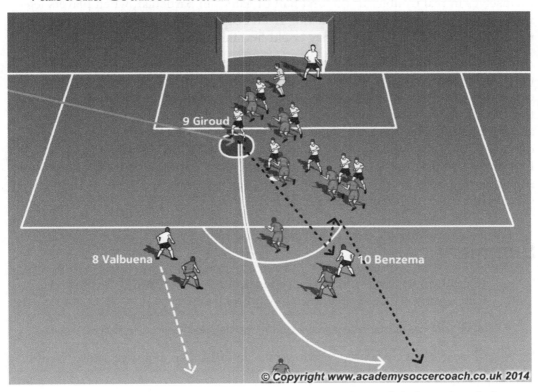

France set up to defend a Swiss corner with all 11 players in and around the box, nine of whom were in the penalty area, with attackers Valbuena and Benzema positioned on the edge. France's third attacking player, Giroud, took up a zonal-marking position on the edge of the six-yard box. It was Giroud who won the header, and began the counter-attack with his subsequent long, quick dash forward. His header landed at Benzema's feet, who 'set' to Raphael Varane to play a long pass behind the Swiss defence for the forward run of Giroud. The move ended with Giroud in Switzerland's penalty area - squaring the ball for Valbuena who had also burst forward from his defensive position, to score from close range. It took less than 14 seconds from the point the ball met Giroud's head to the point it ended up in the Swiss goal.

Limitations to Counter-Attacking from Deep

There is always a high sense of risk for teams playing counter-attacking football from deep. Allowing your opponents free entry to the edge of your defensive third can obviously be very dangerous. Teams need to ensure they defend compactly, with organisation, with discipline, and limit the errors they make. Teams may even do all these things correctly but be undone by quality forward play or by a piece of individual magic.

It was noticeable in Brazil that those teams who did set up to defend deep and counter had a certain window to capitalise – and once this window shut, they found themselves in real trouble. In the first half of games in particular, when players legs were still fresh, teams counter-attacking from deep actually created better chances than their rival due to the space they could find behind the opposition's defence.

Algeria's fixture against Germany early in the tournament was a great example of this. The Africans missed a host of great opportunities in the first half and were eventually made to pay. As the game progressed (it eventually went into extra-time), they physically ran out of steam and ultimately succumbed to German possession and penetration. Had they have taken one of their early chances, they may have had enough in the tank to hold out for an unlikely win. Switzerland suffered the same fate and ended up being eliminated by Argentina in the Round of 16. Had both the Algerians and Swiss been able to score from their golden chances, we would have seen a completely different World Cup Final.

Summary

- In contrast to the South African tournament in 2010, the 2014 World Cup will be remembered for attacking play and goals.

- A World Cup equalling record of 171 goals were scored in Brazil.

- More goals were scored by substitutes in 2014 than at any previous World Cup competition.

- The time period from minute 60 into injury-time was the most profitable for scoring goals.

- Teams who scored first tended to win games, although the early games in Brazil threatened to contradict this trend.

- 80% of goals came from one or two-touch finishes, and almost 90% from inside the penalty box.

- Zone 14 still contributes highly to goal assists.

- The number and significance of goals from set-pieces at the 2014 World Cup was noticeable.

- Players tend to score from decisive shoot-out penalties that will put them through. They tend to miss when elimination is at stake.

- Counter-attacking and attacking transitions have become an important part of teams' attacking armouries.

- Counter-attacking from deep can see teams create *better* chances – but they suffer if they do not take these chances.

- More goals are scored from counter-pressing and regaining possession in attacking areas than regaining the ball in deeper areas of the pitch.

8

A Case for the Defence

"0-0 is the perfect result because it is the expression of total balance between the attack and defence of both teams." (Annibale Frossi, former Italian coach)

As the 2010 World Cup will live in the memory for many as being a rather cautious tournament, its 2014 counterpart will be remembered as day-after-day of thrilling games. There was joyous attacking play, superb goals, great skills, and gallant defeats for Chile, the US, Mexico, Nigeria and Algeria in the first knock-out phase of the tournament alone.

Amidst all the attacking play in Brazil, there were also very interesting patterns in how teams defended. Defending can be a somewhat thankless task. You can defend well for over an hour-and-a-half, and then receive a sucker punch. Just ask Iran how they felt when, with their whole team camped in (and around) their own penalty area, Lionel Messi popped up to score an injury-time winner.

Team defending tactics varied in Brazil, from the high, aggressive press to those who defended deep. Others, like the Dutch used aggressive pressing somewhere in-between the two styles, both of which we will look at in detail here. Although styles and defensive tactics vary from team to team, just like they do offensively, they are governed by key 'rules'.

Chapter 8

Principles of Play

An important preamble to our chapter on defending is to recognise the principles of defending. Regardless of how a team organises itself defensively, it has got to abide by the defending principles of play to be successful. It does not matter what formation a team plays, or what players they employ, the principles remain the same.

Defending Principles of Play[1]

1. Press or Delay	The first consideration, when defending, is whether the team can put pressure on the ball or whether they need to drop off, delay the attack, and reorganise.
2. Support	While the first defender makes the decision about whether to press or delay, his immediate team-mates will look at *what support he needs* and *where*. If the attacker evades the first defender, the second and third defenders can form a secondary barrier between the ball and goal.
3. Balance	'Balance' players are players that are positioned on the 'weak' side of the attack. So, if the attack is building on the left, the attacking players on the right hand side are less of a priority.
4. Compactness	While attacking, players 'disperse' in possession, defending teams attempt to remain 'compact'. By achieving compactness, defenders try to reduce attempts to penetrate the defence.
5. Discipline	There may be times when defending can be stressful and challenging. Any ill-discipline and rash decision-making, especially in and around the box, can lead to attackers exploiting gaps, or the concession of penalty-kicks, free-kicks, etc.

It has often been said that football is a game of space. Increasing the space you have to play in, when attacking, locks horns with an opposition which is looking to reduce the playing space whilst defending. This is, largely, what the game's principles of play are built around, and what governs player movements on the pitch. When teams are then forced to transition quickly, we see sudden shifts from teams and players in dispersed formations to teams trying to become immediately compact. The game, one might suggest, mirrors the playing of the accordion when

---

[1] Taken from *Making the Ball Roll – A Complete Guide to Youth Football For the Aspiring Soccer Coach*

transitioning. This contrast between the white attacking team, and black defending team can be seen below.

In Possession Dispersal v. Out of Possession Compactness

In possession, the white team have spread out to support the player on the ball and to attack. The full-backs, centre-backs and attackers have stretched the playing area vertically and horizontally, while the midfield players look for any spaces that this dispersal has created.

The black team who are defending, however, are looking to remain compact and defend the smallest space possible. With the ball on their right-hand side, the left sided players 'tuck in', knowing that their direct opponent, furthest away from the ball, cannot affect the game in that moment. Should the ball be switched to the other side of the pitch, they know they will have the time to get across and defend this weak side.

In the above graphic, the blacks are out of possession and are defending when organised. In transition however, this level of organisation is not always possible – but teams are required to defend nonetheless.

Defensive Transitions

We introduced the concept of transitions in the previous chapter, and looked at how teams counter-attacked and looked to capitalise on the opposition's defensive disorganisation once they won the ball back. Like any duel, each offensive transition will see the other team in defensive transition – that is, looking to defend immediately having lost possession.

It is arguably much easier to analyse defensive transitions when they have gone wrong. Instances of poor defending can stand out more under analysis and it can spark useful discussions on the methods needed to put them right.

Germany 7 Brazil 1

One of the lasting memories of the 2014 World Cup was Brazil's humiliating defeat on home soil against a rampant, ruthless German side. This type of result between two very strong nations is rare during an international friendly, let alone in the semi-final of the globe's biggest international football event. Statistically, the result is a complete outlier – a one-off that is highly unlikely to reoccur. But occur it did.

Brazil received plenty of criticism during the summer of 2014, even before this game. They were accused of prioritising functionality over flamboyance and essentially playing in a very un-Brazilian manner. But never had we witnessed something like this, nor can anyone truly say they predicted what was to unfold against Germany.

Defensively, and particularly in the defensive transition phase, Brazil were a shambles that evening. The psychological effect of being stripped bare and taking a footballing beating in front of the world in their own back yard contributed as much as tactical disorganisation did to their hammering in Belo Horizonte.

The ideal situation for defending is when a team is *organised*. Organisation means that the defending principles of play are present and correct. Teams will press the ball or will 'drop-off' and prevent forward passes. Support and balance players will be in place creating 'compact' units, and defenders will have the composure to be disciplined in order to make better, clearer, less complicated decisions. We often hear commentators talk about "two banks of four" – a common example of a team playing 4-4-2 and defending with organisation.

Defending in an organised fashion for 90 minutes or more, however, is impossible – regardless of a team's formation, set up or system. There will be points in the game where disorganisation occurs, and teams may even become outnumbered in defensive areas. At this point other defending skills are required; delaying attacks, making recovery runs, or forcing the play into a less dangerous area. During transition phases, having just surrendered possession, teams need to recover and either become organised or simply do whatever is necessary to prevent the opposition scoring.

Teams that are disorganised when defending can be quite obvious. Players and units are not only out of position, but can appear out of control and sometimes quite desperate. The sheer Brazilian panic once Germany entered attacking areas was very noticeable that night, as we will see from Brazil's poor defensive transition below.

Germany's Fourth Goal v. Brazil

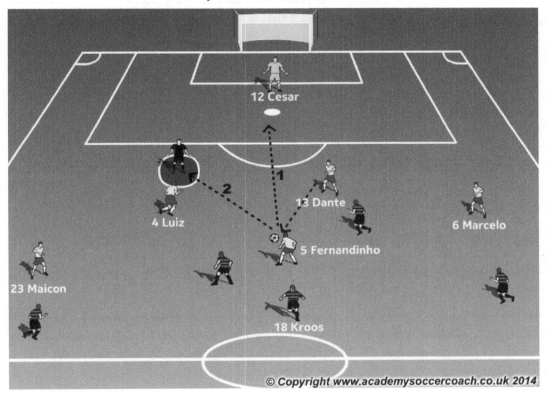

Once Dante played the pass into Fernandinho, Kroos and Germany saw their opportunity to press. Kroos ultimately won the ball back and Germany went on to score. An excellent attacking transition goal from a German point of view.

From a Brazilian viewpoint, however, this typified their poor transitions throughout the game, and we can pinpoint several errors. While still in possession, Fernandinho has one option, even amidst Germany's aggressive press – to use goalkeeper Julio César as a passing option to relieve the pressure. David Luiz should be an option for him also, had he 'dispersed' correctly into the position in the shaded area, with his body facing the rest of the pitch.

Maicon should have seen the transition coming once Fernandinho did not use César and begun to recover in an attempt to become compact, as should have Marcelo. By the time Germany enter the box, Fernandinho and Dante are left exposed, and the others, even the heavily criticized Luiz, were unable or unwilling to recover quickly enough. Khedira and Kroos even had the time to exchange passes before putting the ball in the net. A successful defensive transition would not allow this.

There are many, many other cases of poor defensive transitions during the 2014 World Cup. With the U.S.A. beating Portugal 2 – 1 in injury time, when a win would have made their passage beyond the group stage more comfortable, they were in possession near Portugal's corner flag – and the ball as far away from their goal as it could be. The U.S. surrendered this possession and seconds later Portugal had raced to the other end and equalised against a shamefully disorganised team. I am sure coach Jürgen Klinsmann was furious.

There were of course thousands and thousands of good defensive transitions. Javier Mascherano's excellent individual performance in the semi-final against the Netherlands, for example, saw his last ditch recoveries and tackles send Argentina into the Final.

Javier Mascherano Defensive Total 2014 World Cup Statistics

Tackles	30
Interceptions	18
Clearances	13
Fouls Committed	10 (one yellow card)

Mascherano was key to Argentina's defensive transition in his role as holding central midfielder. Although excellent on the ball also (a key trait of a modern midfielder), his defensive statistics stack up against any other individual in Brazil and were a central factor to Argentina's excellent defensive numbers.

You may even say that a defensive transition was successful any time a team defended a counter-attack without conceding. Think back to Neuer and how many times he was called to sweep up Algerian attacks during their Round of 16 fixture. When the Africans attacked quickly, once the Germans lost possession, Neuer's role as sweeper-keeper in transition was crucial for the success of Germany's high-pressure defensive tactics.

High Pressing

Teams that use a high-pressure tactic look to engage the opposition as far up the pitch as is possible. They hope to regain the ball early and as near to the opponent's goal as possible. As Johan Cruyff succinctly put it, "when you win the ball back, there are 30 metres to goal, rather than 80." When done well, the pressing team moves together with intensity, aiming to capitalise on their opponent's poor technique or dispersing movements. When it is done very well, it is very difficult to play against.

Pressing opponents in attacking areas proved both very popular and very productive for teams at the 2014 World Cup. As we looked at in the previous chapter (we have included the graph again below), Germany scored 70% of their goals from regaining the ball back in their opponents' defensive areas, and in total the competition saw just over 42% of the goals scored from regains in this third of the pitch, and over 60% if we include the whole of the opposition's half.

Areas of Pitch Where Ball is Regained Leading to a Goal at the 2014 World Cup

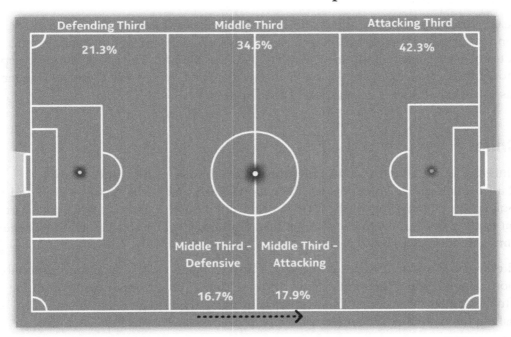

© Copyright www.academysoccercoach.co.uk 2014

By splitting the pitch into thirds, and tracking the number of regains that resulted in a goal, we see that most goals (over 42%) came from winning the ball in the attacking third. This number decreases as we work back through the pitch, where regaining the ball in defensive areas resulted in just over 21% of the goals.

This high press, or counter-press, is the product of analysis and a certain pragmatism towards the game. Although we all love free-flowing passing moves that result in goals (who can forget Esteban Cambiasso's goal in the 2006 World Cup for Argentina against Serbia after a move involving 24 passes) the reality is that the overwhelming majority of goals come from passing sequences of five passes or less. So while we look at possession as being an exclusively offensive tactic, the greatest asset in being able to keep the ball may well be a defensive one. Having possession starves the opposition of the ball, reducing their opportunities to attack and score. Spain and Barcelona's recent ability to keep the ball for defensive reasons saw the style given the nickname 'passenaccio', a pun of the ultra-defensive *catenaccio* tactic made famous by Inter Milan and coach Helenio Herrera in the 1960s.

By using a high press, teams make a concerted effort to win the ball back higher up the pitch, meaning that they can attack quickly and look to score within a handful of passes. They will look to capitalise on poor technique or bad decisions from the opposition, or try to regain the ball in transition before their opponent is organised or in controlled possession.

Teams that press high need to do so in groups, and as a team[2], in an effort to condense the space the opposition have to play in. The *intensity* of the tactic is vital as teams try to unsettle opposing players who have the ball. The intent is to intercept should the opponent try to play out using short passes, or to force them into longer passes that are easier to regain possession from.

Chile

Chilean football and its identity will forever be indebted to innovative coach Marcelo Bielsa. The Argentine was the nation's head coach from 2007 to 2011 and took charge of the group at the 2010 World Cup in South Africa. Following a short but fruitless spell under another Argentine, Claudio Borghi, a third Argentine, Jorge Sampaoli, took charge and reinvented their modern trademark style.

There is no doubting Bielsa's influence on Sampaoli and Chile's newfound national footballing identity. Their defensive intent was to press their opponent high up the pitch, by either intercepting short passes, or forcing them to give the ball away by making them attempt longer passes. Chile refused to let teams settle when they are in possession.

---

[2] Below, we will look at the effects of a team's pressing tactics when the whole group is not in sync.

Their Round of 16 fixture against Brazil, which they ultimately lost after a penalty shoot-out, was a case in point. The Chileans went behind early in the game after David Luiz prodded in a corner-kick at the back post, but equalised later in the half – a goal that ultimately took them into extra-time.

A Brazil throw-in, in their own defensive third, saw the Chileans push bodies forward, aiming to 'trap' the Brazilians, and hoping to win back possession. Marcelo's throw-in, and Hulk's subsequent attempt to play a pass first time, saw his poor touch hounded by Vargas. Now, in attacking transition just outside the box, Vargas fed strike partner Alexis Sánchez whose finish was clinical to make the score 1 – 1. Within seconds, Brazil went from having possession with a throw-in, to conceding possession and conceding a goal.

Earlier in the competition, Chile met Spain. Although all eyes were on Spain after their watershed 5 – 1 defeat to the Netherlands, it was the Chileans who grabbed the attention. Chile, who again pressed aggressively and high up the pitch, once again exposed Spanish tiki-taka and completed a comfortable 2 – 0 win.

Chile's High Press Against Spain

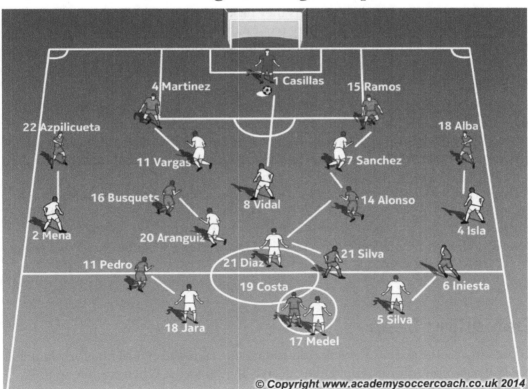

© Copyright www.academysoccercoach.co.uk 2014

Spain's tiki-taka style in recent years saw them attempt to start attacks from the back, with the goalkeeper. Against Chile, with goalkeeper Casillas in possession, the South Americans would press. All outfield players would press to compact the space Spain had to play in. In the image above, Vidal pressed Casillas, Sánchez got into position to cover the pass to Alonso, while ready to press Sergio Ramos. Díaz screened Silva and also picked up Alonso if Spain could work the ball past Sánchez.

Dangers of the High Press

If the high pressing tactic was so successful, and so difficult to play against, the most obvious question is why doesn't everyone do it? The answer could be as simple as the reasons why certain teams don't play possession football, or don't play with a back three – not every team can cope with the high demands and often high risk of the pressing game.

It is extremely difficult to play a high pressure game for over 90 minutes, never mind doing so when games go into extra-time. Even Chile struggled in extra-time against Brazil and dropped back to play on the counter-attack. Players need to be physically fit, but also disciplined in the decisions they make when committing to pressing the ball. Once they regain possession, they require the technical skills to be able to maintain the ball and hurt the opposition with quick play, and clever and penetrating passes. Out of possession, pressing teams need to be able to recover quickly, and protect any space they leave in behind them.

In Germany's case, goalkeeper Manuel Neuer played an important role in defending the space behind his back four to allow his team to press high up the pitch, constantly leaving his penalty area to sweep up passes in behind his defence. This was most notable in Germany's last 16 game against Algeria. Although the tactic met with lots of scrutiny as pundits felt the tactic was too edge-of-your-seat dangerous, the role of Neuer in Germany's pressing game was calculated and a requirement of the team's style of play, especially against Algeria who were determined to defend deep. This danger was again present in the first half of their quarter-final against France, although tactical alterations saw the Germans sit deeper in the second period to see out a 1 – 0 victory.

Defending Deep

If pressing can be seen as proactive defending (i.e. taking responsibility for winning the ball back yourself) then defending deep is the opposite. When you set up to defend deep you are defending *re-actively*, happy to allow the opposition possession of the ball - reactive to their decisions.

Teams normally defend deep when they are technically inferior to the opposition, or if they are attempting to hold on to a lead or claim a draw. At the beginning of the chapter we noted how difficult it is to maintain a perfect defensive strategy. Throughout the competition teams like Iran, Switzerland, Greece and Algeria were all examples of sides who, through their inferiority to their opposition, attempted to retreat and delay opponent attacks once they lost possession of the ball. There are many examples of this done well, but also many examples of the tactic being undone.

Iran

Prior to the World Cup Finals, very few fancied the Iranians to cause a stir in Brazil. Marshalled by Portuguese coach Carlos Queiroz, their tactics were heavily based on defending deep, and freely allowing the opposition to take possession of the ball. Whether Iran were out to win games, or just make themselves known at international level is hard to say. Queiroz will undoubtedly say that there was sufficient intent to counter-attack and win games in this manner, although throughout their three games, this was difficult to see.

Bosnia was their biggest defeat, beaten 3 – 1 with just 33.9% of the ball. Against Argentina they were a whisker away from a claiming a nil-nil draw with 21.2% possession. They did manage a goalless draw against the Nigerians, their only positive result at the World Cup, with less than a third of possession (30.4%).

Iran's Defensive 4-2-3-1 in 0 – 0 Draw v. Nigeria

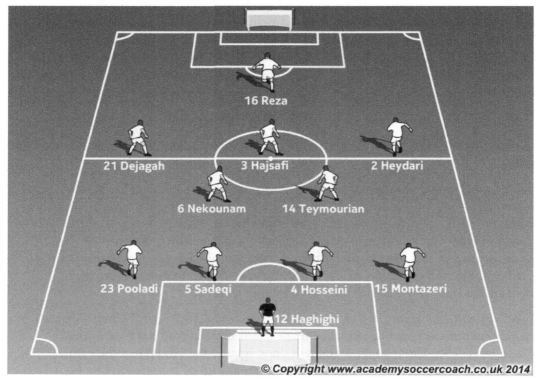

Lining up in a 4-2-3-1 formation, this often became a 4-1-4-1 or a 4-4-1-1 for Iran. The shape changed in reaction to the opposition's forward runs or the pressure they started to pile on the Iranians. In chapter five, we looked at a visual of Messi's winning goal against them, where all eleven players were in or around the box, and how their set formation was obliterated by group compactness in a desperate desire to hold on to win.

When teams are defending deep their main focus is on defending the goal and the central areas in front of goal. They attempt to lure the opposition out of shape and counter-attack once they are disorganised. Teams defending deep will look to force the opposition into playing longer passes, limit them to passing side-to-side in front of them, or force the ball and the attack into wider, less dangerous areas.

Defending With Ten Men

We noted earlier in this chapter that a team is at its most comfortable defensively when they are organised. The team as a whole, and the units within it, will be compact and in control, even without the ball. This pre-planned organisation will be ruined however when faced with a sending off and playing with a man down. In total, there were ten red cards shown in Brazil (seven fewer than in 2010). All ten cards went to players from different teams.

Teams that are forced into action with ten men, especially those already in the lead and with something to hold on to, will defend deep in an effort to hold on to the advantage they have. Adding a second goal will largely come as a result of counter-attacks that tend to become less and less frequent as the overworked players grow fatigued.

Costa Rica – Greece

In the 52nd minute of this Round of 16 fixture, Costa Rica took the lead thanks to a left-footed strike from captain Bryan Ruiz. In the 66th minute, however, centre-back Oscar Duarte picked up his second booking, was subsequently sent off, and the whole shape of the game changed. Costa Rica were a man down, but a goal up, and needed to hold on – and hold on they very nearly did.

The sending off brought about changes from both sides. Costa Rica began defending deeper, desperate to hang on to their one-goal lead. They were literally playing out time. Greek coach Fernando Santos, meanwhile, introduced forward Theofanis Gekas and began to pile pressure on the Central Americans with a front diamond and his full-backs pushing into attack. The pressure was ultimately decisive, but only in the dying seconds of injury-time, as Sokratis Papastathopoulos drove home from close range following a spill from the otherwise excellent goalkeeper Keylor Navas.

Navas was called into action frequently during extra-time as the trend of Greek attacks and deep Costa Rican defending continued. At the other end, against a tiring frontline, Greek goalkeeper Orestis Karnezis was not required to make a single save. Although they could not hold out in normal time, Costa Rica were able to do so for the entire 30 minutes of extra-time. This team ethic and belief in their changed tactic was admirable, especially considering the psychological blow they were dealt from conceding in the 91st minute of normal time. Their resolute defending with 10 men gave them the platform to secure a win via a penalty shoot-out.

Costa Rica Defending With Ten Men v. Greece

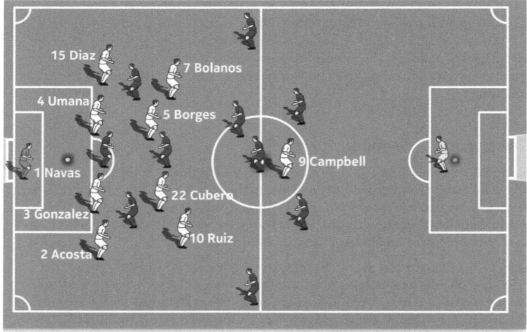

© Copyright www.academysoccercoach.co.uk 2014

Upon the sending off of Duarte, Costa Rica changed from their 5-at-the-back shape to a back four; they defended deep, and relied on the attacking forages of Joel Campbell or Bryan Ruiz. The Costa Ricans remained compact defensively, and were happy to give up possession in an effort to cling on to their single goal advantage.

When to Press and When to Drop

There was a wonderful moment in the 37th minute of the Last 16 game between Brazil and Chile. This was not a goal, a foul, a chance or anything that will feature on the game's highlight reels. But it was a fantastic example of the tactical understanding of when it is possible to press or to drop off.

As we know, Chile like to press aggressively, but they also acknowledge and realise when the press is not possible. With Thiago Silva in possession from a Dani Alves throw-in on the edge of Brazil's penalty area, Chile's trigger for the press began. The closest Chilean player, Alexis Sánchez, moved towards Silva. He even turned his head before his press to see if Vidal was in a position to press with him (Vidal was in position, but chose not to press). Instead of Vidal, Sánchez was backed up by midfielder Marcelo Díaz (normally the deepest of Chile's midfield, but he found himself high up the pitch on this occasion). To relieve the pressure, Silva passed square to centre-back partner David Luiz. Realising that he could not get pressure on the ball due to the large distance between himself and Luiz, and that Vidal was not pressing, Díaz dramatically put the brakes on and retreated, dropping back into his deep midfield position. His arms even flailed in the air - almost cartoon-like - as he changed from aggressive pressing into necessary dropping!

Over the last decade, the national team that grabbed all our attention (and almost all the trophies) with a tactic of this kind of high, early and aggressive press was Spain. Pressing however requires – as the instance above with Chile shows – that the whole team reacts appropriately. Either you press in numbers, or you drop off.

If a player can get pressure on the ball, your defenders can squeeze up the pitch, reducing the space and giving the opposition less room to play in. However, if a team's defensive line steps up *without* pressure on the ball, you will leave space in behind your defence that can be exposed by longer or penetrative passes. The Netherland's first goal against Spain, as illustrated below, shows the problems that a defence can face when they leave space in behind them without there being adequate pressure on the ball.

Spain's Defending Solutions for van Persie Goal

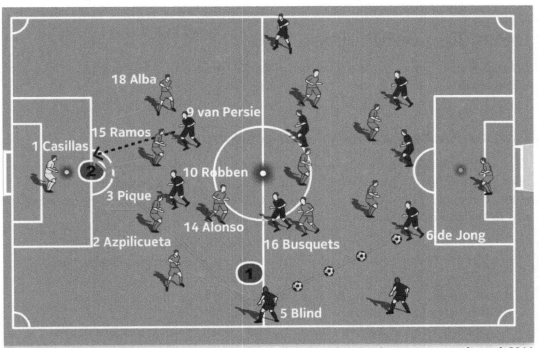

Without any pressure on the ball, Dutch wing-back Daley Blind has the opportunity to receive, get his head up and play a longer pass into the space behind Spanish centre-backs Gerard Piqué and an out-of-position Sergio Ramos, and in front of oncoming striker Robin van Persie. It leaves

goalkeeper Iker Casillas exposed as he rushes into no-man's land to defend the exposed space.
Casillas' efforts were ultimately defeated by an expertly taken header from van Persie.

As the ball transfers from de Jong to Blind, we normally expect 'this' Spanish team to press aggressively through either Azpilicueta or Busquets, or normally both (greyed option 1). Busquets can leave the opponent he is closest to as his deepest midfield colleague, Xabi Alonso, is there to cover any forward run. Azpilicueta and Busquets can outnumber Blind, and box him in with the aid of the touchline. Their intent would be to regain possession from Blind themselves, or force him backwards.

This press however did not happen. With no pressure on Blind, Spain's back four and Casillas needed to protect the space between them from the runs of Robben and van Persie (greyed area 2). Both Piqué and Ramos needed to drop, and Alba needed to provide cover. Casillas needed to be aware of the space in front of him. All the principles of defensive play needed to be applied!

So, in this instance Spain neither got pressure on the ball, nor did their defenders drop off. Ultimately, the side was exposed.

Defending Set-Pieces

With the importance of goals from set-pieces (examined at in the previous chapter), teams spend lots of time formulating ways to defend them.

Corner-Kicks – Zonal v. Man-Marking

Zonal marking at corner-kicks is often chastised as being ineffective, especially from television pundits. Napoli's Head Coach, Rafael Benitez, is a firm believer in the tactic, however. Using data from his time at Liverpool on his website, Benitez had this to say about the effectiveness of zonal marking:

> *"it (the data) shows that it should not be the system that is blamed for conceding*
> *goals at set-pieces but it will always depend on the determination, concentration and*
> *ability in the air of the players at the moment of delivery of the set-piece. The data*
> *certainly does not show that one system will always be better than the other. It is*
> *about using the right system for the right players at the right time. In fact, at*
> *Liverpool the zonal marking evolved through the years … to take into consideration*
> *the changes in personnel of the team, but still maintained the high success rate."*

Five of the six seasons when 'Rafa' was at Liverpool, the Merseyside club were in the bottom four for conceding from corner-kicks.

Switzerland Zonal Marking From Corners

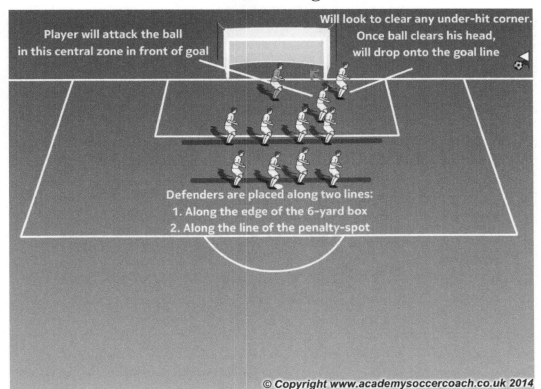

The essence of zonal marking is that players take up a space and will attack the ball should it come into 'their' space. The two lines also make up two barriers where players look to block the runs of attackers. Once the ball is delivered into a zone, it is the responsibility of that player to clear.

Mixed-Marking

I intentionally misled you when I wrote the title of the above section. The heading, "Zonal v. Man-Marking", suggests that there is a conflict between both, or that one way is better than another. This comparison has probably been over-analysed for far too long, when the truth is that the vast majority of teams defend corners using a combination of both.

Designated man-markers, normally those with the best aerial attributes, are designated to mark the biggest, most dangerous opponents. Those in zonal areas are placed there as they are high-risk areas, where a body is needed to thwart the chances of scoring. Most commonly, zonal players will be found in an area screening the near post area, on the edge of the six-yard box, and the edge of the penalty box.

Russia Mixed-Marking v. South Korea

Like most teams, Russia used a defending corner system that involved designated man-markers and designated players who took up zonal positions (Z1, Z2 and Z3).

In the previous chapter, we analysed France and Valbuena's wonderful counter-attack goal from defending a corner-kick. Like Russia, France defended with all eleven players in defensive positions. Argentina however, defended corners with only nine players. Such tactics often boil down to a coach's philosophy.

Argentina Defend Corner With Nine Players v. Bosnia

Similarly to Russia, Argentina used a mix of zonal and man-marking when defending corners. However, against Bosnia, coach Sabella was happy to defend with only nine outfield players. To ensure they could defend against a counter-attack, Bosnia were 'forced' to defend with three players against Agüero and Messi. Defending a corner, but leaving two strikers at the halfway line, meant that Argentina did not use any defenders on the posts.

You will notice, not just from the Argentina/Bosnia game, but also from all the diagrams above, that a common theme throughout was not to defend with players assigned to each post. Traditionally, placing players (usually smaller ones) on each post was common, designed to clear any efforts on goal that were out of the reach of the goalkeeper. Only Iran consistently had players marking both posts at the World Cup, and a splattering of teams defended with either one player at the back or the front post.

The reasons for these tactical decisions can be wide and varied. They often depend on the philosophy of the coach, what risk his is willing to take, and player-centred coaches will also consult their goalkeeper and his preferences. Modern goalkeepers are generally happy to take more responsibility for defending their whole goal line, and indeed their whole goal area.

Teams that defend corners with one or no players marking the posts can use these 'extra' players to compete and stop teams winning the first header. This in turn reduces the chance for the opposition to get a shot on goal at all, thus negating the need for players on the posts. Should a team threaten the goal, the players that adopt screening zonal positions near the front post often drop onto the line if the corner goes over their head. We also see more teams being caught offside once the ball is cleared and quickly re-delivered into the goal area.

Summary

- All defending, regardless of individual team tactics, is governed by the defending principles of play.

- Because transitions to counter-attack are a major tactic, being able to transition defensively becomes very important.

- Brazil's shortcomings in this department against Germany are a great example of this.

- Javier Mascherano's role in the Argentine team was vital in how they transitioned successfully.

- Teams like Chile used a high pressing tactic to win the ball back nearer to their opponent's goal.

- Done without proper team and unit organisation, high pressing can be dangerous.

- Teams who are a goal up, or who feel inferior to the opposition, may choose to defend deep.

- Iran defended deep and resolutely in a 4-2-3-1 and had only 33.9%, 21.2% and 30.4% possession respectively in their three World Cup games.

- Tactics will change when teams are forced to play with 10 men. Costa Rica defended resolutely for an hour with 10 in their victory over Greece.

- Regardless of team tactics, all teams must make situational decisions about whether to press the ball, or whether to drop off.

- With the number of set-piece goals at the World Cup, especially from corner kicks, teams must have a strategy for defending them.

- Most teams mixed man-marking with zonal-marking and used either one player or no player marking the goalposts.

- Switzerland defended corners zonally, Iran with a player on each post, and Argentina with just nine players.

9
Conclusion

"One of the best World Cups ever, especially due to the diversity of tactics, styles, and philosophies." (Mark Wotte, Dutch Football Coach; Performance Director, Scottish FA)

The 2014 World Cup was great. We saw attacking games, upsets, last-minute goals, penalty shoot-outs and some big teams leaving the competition early. We even saw the soap opera of football capturing headlines with the Luis Suárez biting incident, national mourning for Neymar's horrific back injury, and (of course) the demolition of the host nation by Germany in 'their' World Cup.

Entertainment and soap operas aside, from a tactical point of view the 2014 World Cup was even better.

Systems

Modern football tactics constantly evolve. Following the South African World Cup in 2010, where 4-2-3-1 was a staple, the 2014 version threw up some real tactical variation. Although 4-2-3-1 was common, we saw the return of familiar and unfamiliar 4-4-2s, the presence of 4-3-3, and 4-5-1, and a number of teams based around teams playing with three defenders.

Some of these systems were based on national identities, whilst other nations were happy to rip up their footballing blueprint and change the way they play. Traditional systems and playing philosophies were tinkered with, and adjusted, to meet the needs of modern football. We saw variation in terms of coaches choosing players around a particular system, with others penning their best players on the team-sheets first, then building the rest of the team and tactics around them.

Players

If anyone was ever in any doubt about how much football has changed over the past decade or so, the 2014 World Cup should have put all that to bed. Although we see lots of team changes, we were entertained by watching players' roles and responsibilities becoming more interchangeable.

Goalkeepers played outside their penalty area, full-backs saw as much of the attacking half as their defensive one, centre-backs joined attacks, and strikers were almost goal-less. Midfield players showed that now, more than ever, they need to be virtually position-less. Attacking midfielders played anywhere that was required, while defensive midfielders were creative as much as destructive. Those in midfield areas were multi-purpose. They scored the goals, were integral to defensive balance and screening, and played deep, high, right, left and centrally.

Styles

In Brazil, we saw the destruction of Spain's stranglehold on international football. Having won three back-to-back major international tournaments with their possession-based tiki-taka style of play, there were question marks about whether this style and generation of players could make it a fourth. Although Germany won the competition, their possession-game had greater variation to it. Unlike Spain, they had a noticeable plan B and could win games whether they passed short, played direct, used a centre-forward or a false nine – and whether they dominated possession or not.

Playing football *without the ball* may be the biggest tactical trend to come out of the 2014 World Cup. Teams were happy to base their attacking strategy around their defensive organisation and discipline. There was real proof in Brazil that games could be exhilarating, entertaining and fruitful, even when the team does not have the ball! The Netherlands beat Spain comprehensively with much less possession, while Algeria very nearly upset the eventual champions Germany playing on the counter-attack.

Attack and Defend

If South Africa 2010 was remembered for displays that focused on not being beaten, its 2014 cousin was very much about risk-taking, with the majority of teams out to win games and score goals. The group stages of the competition were very fruitful in terms of how many goals were scored, and although the knock-out stages produced an average decrease in goals per game (aside from the 7-1 defeat of Brazil by Germany), we were entertained by several teams being defeated gallantly, gaining plaudits along the way. The 120 minutes of football between the Netherlands and Costa Rica was one of the most entertaining of the competition, although the game finished 0-0, and even discounting the usual drama of penalty shoot-outs and a strange late substitution from Louis van Gaal.

The proliferation of counter-attacking goals and the focus on defensive and attacking transitions was clear for all to see, and focusing on these transitions may be where the future of football lies – only the 2018 World Cup will tell us for sure!

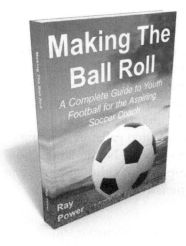

★★★★★ ▾ (19)

(Amazon.co.uk Sep 2014)

Making The Ball Roll: A Complete Guide to Youth Football for the Aspiring Soccer Coach by Ray Power

Making the Ball Roll is the ultimate complete guide to coaching youth soccer.

This focused and easy-to-understand book details training practices and tactics, and goes on to show you how to help young players achieve peak performance through tactical preparation, communication, psychology, and age-specific considerations. Each chapter covers, in detail, a separate aspect of coaching to give you, the football coach, a broad understanding of youth soccer development. Each topic is brought to life by the stories of real coaches working with real players. Never before has such a comprehensive guide to coaching soccer been found in the one place. If you are a new coach, or just trying to improve your work with players - and looking to invest in your future - this is a must-read book!

Soccer Tough by Dan Abrahams

★★★★★ ▾ (57)

(Amazon.co.uk Sep 2014)

"Take a minute to slip into the mind of one of the world's greatest soccer players and imagine a stadium around you. Picture a performance under the lights and mentally play the perfect game."

Technique, speed and tactical execution are crucial components of winning soccer, but it is mental toughness that marks out the very best players – the ability to play when pressure is highest, the opposition is strongest, and fear is greatest. Top players and coaches understand the importance of sport psychology in soccer but how do you actually train your mind to become the best player you can be?

Soccer Tough demystifies this crucial side of the game and offers practical techniques that will enable soccer players of all abilities to actively develop focus, energy, and confidence. Soccer Tough will help banish the fear, mistakes, and mental limits that holds players back.

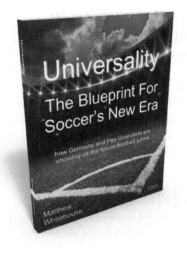

★★★★★ ▾ (1)

(Amazon.co.uk Sep 2014)

Universality | The Blueprint for Soccer's New Era: How Germany and Pep Guardiola are showing us the Future Football Game by Matthew Whitehouse

In this book, Matthew Whitehouse – acclaimed author of The Way Forward: Solutions to England's Football Failings - looks in-depth at the past decade of the game, taking the reader on a journey into football's evolution. Examining the key changes that have occurred since the turn of the century, right up to the present, the book looks at the evolution of tactics, coaching, and position-specific play. They have led us to this moment: to the rise of universality. Published September 2014.

★★★★★ ▾ (28)

(Amazon.co.uk Sep 2014)

Soccer Brain: The 4C Coaching Model for Developing World Class Player Mindsets and a Winning Football Team by Dan Abrahams

Coaching soccer is demanding. Impossible to perfect, it requires a broad knowledge of many performance areas including technique, tactics, psychology and the social aspects of human development. The first two components are covered in detail in many texts – but Soccer Brain uniquely offers a comprehensive guide to developing the latter two – player mindsets and winning teams.

Soccer Brain is for the no limits coach. It's for the coach who is passionate about developing players and building a winning team. This is not a traditional soccer coaching book filled with drills or tactics or playing patterns. This book is about getting the very best from you, the coach, and helping you develop a coaching culture of excellence and world class football mindsets.

★★★★★ ▾ (58)

(Amazon.co.uk Sep 2014)

The Way Forward: Solutions to England's Football Failings
by Matthew Whitehouse

English football is in a state of crisis. It has been almost 50 years since England made the final of a major championship and the national sides, at all levels, continue to disappoint and underperform. Yet no-one appears to know how to improve the situation.

In his acclaimed book, The Way Forward, football coach Matthew Whitehouse examines the causes of English football's decline and offers a number of areas where change and improvement need to be implemented immediately. With a keen focus and passion for youth development and improved coaching he explains that no single fix can overcome current difficulties and that a multi-pronged strategy is needed. If we wish to improve the standards of players in England then we must address the issues in schools, the grassroots, and academies, as well as looking at the constraints of the Premier League and English FA.

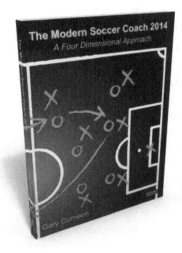

★★★★★ ▾ (32)

(Amazon.co.uk Sep 2014)

The Modern Soccer Coach by Gary Curneen

Aimed at Soccer coaches of all levels and with players of all ages and abilities The Modern Soccer Coach 2014 identifies the areas that must be targeted by coaches who want to maximize a team's potential – the Technical, Tactical, Physical, and Mental sides to the game. See how the game has changed and what areas determine success in the game today. Learn what sets coaches like Mourinho, Klopp, Rodgers, and Guardiola apart from the rest. Philosophies and training methods from the most forward thinking coaches in the game today are presented, along with guidelines on creating a modern environment for readers' teams. This book is not about old school methodologies – it is about creating a culture of excellence that gets the very best from players. Contains more than 30 illustrated exercises that focus on tactical, technical, mental, and physical elements of the game.

★★★★⯪ ▾ (4)

(Amazon.co.uk Sep 2014)

José Mourinho: The Rise of the Translator by Ciaran Kelly

From Porto to Chelsea, and Inter to Real Madrid – the Mourinho story is as intriguing as the man himself. Now, a new challenge awaits at Stamford Bridge. Covering the Mourinho story to October 2013 and featuring numerous exclusive interviews with figures not synonymous with the traditional Mourinho narrative.

"Enlightening interviews with those who really know José Mourinho" – Simon Kuper, Financial Times.

"Superb read from a terrific writer" – Ger McCarthy, Irish Examiner

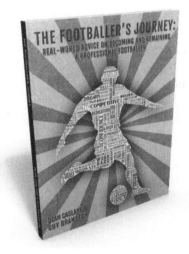

★★★★★ ▾ (5)

(Amazon.co.uk Sep 2014)

The Footballer's Journey: real-world advice on becoming and remaining a professional footballer by Dean Caslake and Guy Branston

Many youngsters dream of becoming a professional footballer. But football is a highly competitive world where only a handful will succeed. Many aspiring soccer players don't know exactly what to expect, or what is required, to make the transition from the amateur world to the 'bright lights' in front of thousands of fans.

The Footballer's Journey maps out the footballer's path with candid insight and no-nonsense advice. It examines the reality of becoming a footballer including the odds of 'making it', how academies really work, the importance of attitude and mindset, and even the value of having a backup plan if things don't quite work out. Filled with real life stories from current, and former, professionals across different leagues.

Other Recent and Forthcoming Books from Bennion Kearny

★★★★★ ▾ (6) (Amazon.co.uk Sep 2014)

What Business Can Learn From Sport Psychology
by Dr Martin Turner & Dr Jamie Barker

★★★★⯪ ▾ (7) (Amazon.co.uk Sep 2014)

The 7 Master Moves of Success
by Jag Shoker

★★★★★ ▾ (9) (Amazon.co.uk Sep 2014)

Saturday Afternoon Fever: A Year On The Road For Soccer Saturday
by Johnny Phillips

★★★★★ ▾ (2) (Amazon.co.uk Sep 2014)

Small Time: A Life in the Football Wilderness
by Justin Bryant

★★★★★ ▾ (2) (Amazon.co.uk Sep 2014)

Conference Season [2012/2013 Season]
by Steve Leach

Coming Soon

What is Tactical Periodization?
by Xavier Tamarit

Lightning Source UK Ltd.
Milton Keynes UK
UKOW07f2216180315

248097UK00006B/41/P

9 781909 125964